# Advance Praise for
# The Case for Dividend Growth

*"In three-decade baby boom retirements, the only rational investment objective isn't income; it's growth of income. Your income has to keep rising on at least the same trajectory as your living costs, or you'll run out of money. No problem: the dividends of mainstream equities have, in the aggregate, been increasing at almost twice CPI inflation for as long as any of us have been alive. And wait, there's more: to the extent you can live on those rising dividends, your patrimony can continue to grow for your heirs. Yet it isn't too much to say that the immense power of dividend growth has always been the least understood, most underappreciated phenomenon in investing. Well, not anymore: investors of all ages will find David Bahnsen's pellucid and highly readable tutorial a life-forwarding experience."*

—NICK MURRAY, author of *Simple Wealth, Inevitable Wealth*

*"David's understanding of capital markets comes through in this book loud and clear. From alternatives to fixed income, to the asset class that is the subject of this book, dividend stocks, he writes in a way that allows investors of all shapes and sizes to understand. You'll be a better investor for reading."*

—ANTHONY SCARAMUCCI, Founder and CEO, SkyBridge Capital

*"In a financial world of pundits and experts energized by prediction compulsion, David Bahnsen stands out as an advisor who understands and embraces the eternal truth that long term accumulation and reinvestment of dividend income is the major key to sustainable investment success."*

—LOWELL MILLER, Chief Investment Officer and Co-founder, Miller/Howard Investments

*"Throughout his successful career, David has implemented a consistent dividend growth equity investment philosophy. In this book, David provides the reader valuable new insight toward that process in a coherent, unique and thoughtful manner. Readers will become more complete investors after understanding David's dividend growth philosophy."*

—JOSEPH M. TERRANOVA, Senior Managing Director, Virtus Investment Partners; CNBC Ensemble Member since 2008

## Also by David L. Bahnsen

**Crisis of Responsibility:**
Our Cultural Addiction to Blame and How You Can Cure It

the case for

# DIVIDEND GROWTH

INVESTING IN A POST-CRISIS WORLD

the case for

# DIVIDEND GROWTH

INVESTING IN A POST-CRISIS WORLD

DAVID L. BAHNSEN

A POST HILL PRESS BOOK

The Case for Dividend Growth:
Investing in a Post-Crisis World
© 2019 by David L. Bahnsen
All Rights Reserved

ISBN: 978-1-64293-045-0
ISBN (eBook): 978-1-64293-046-7

Cover art by Cody Corcoran
Interior Design and Composition by Greg Johnson/Textbook Perfect

Published in association with the literary agency of Legacy, LLC,
501 N. Orlando Avenue, Suite #313-348, Winter Park, FL 32789.

David and his team of investment professionals, the Bahnsen Group LLC,
are registered with HighTower Advisors, LLC. The opinions expressed in
this book are David's and do not represent those of HighTower or its affil-
iates. This is not an offer to buy or sell securities, and HighTower shall
not in any way be liable for claims related to this writing, and makes no
expressed or implied representations or warranties as to its accuracy or
completeness.

**Post Hill Press**
New York · Nashville
posthillpress.com

Published in the United States of America

*For Darin Dennee, whose friendship from 1996–2001*
*provided some of the greatest memories, laughs,*
*and catalysts for growth any human could ever hope for,*
*and who shares my belief in a life of aspiration.*
*It is from those aspirations that this book is born.*
*May your life always receive the dividends*
*you so richly deserve.*

# CONTENTS

The first ten years of this new millennium provided an exciting opportunity for investor education—it provided a "lost decade" in U.S. equities. Book-ended by two massive bear markets, just as the demographic reality of baby boomer retirements began, investors were given a chance to remember what investing is supposed to be about, and what can lead to disaster. Through the turbulent first decade of this new millennium, and the post-financial crisis reality since, the assumptions that drive investor behavior and decisions have been challenged, and hopefully informed. And from the decades that pre-dated this new millennium, and everything we have seen since, one thing stands out.... Dividend growth investing represents a mathematical miracle that creates an offense and a defense for savvy investors that stands the test of time.

The investment industry has convinced us that there are "growth" investors, and there are "income" investors; there are "conservative" investors, and "aggressive" ones. But the fact of the matter is, with all the different nuances in risk appetite, timeline, personality, sophistication, and anything else, all objectives and descriptions end up coming down to one thing…a receipt of cash. The rest is just details.

There was a time when dividends were half, or more, of the annual return stocks offered. But as dividend yields have dropped across broad equity indices, are we to believe that price appreciation will be substantially higher than its historical average, to equal past total returns? In reality, companies that have stood the test of time become dividend payers. Technology is proving this true of entire sectors. The past and future are about companies rewarding their shareholders with profits paid out as cash. And in studying the history of this, we learn a lot we need to know about the future.

Yes, the dividend is cash we put in our pocket. Yes, the dividend is a continued and realized form of reward (compensation) in exchange for the investment made into the company. But what too many miss is not what the dividend does for us as investors, but what the dividend tells us about the company we own. Shareholder alignment with management matters. And so does the "tell" of a cash payment in a world of crazy accounting.

Before we talk about the advantage of dividends for those withdrawing from their wealth, we need to look at the equally potent force of people using dividends to accumulate wealth. That accumulation story causes us to look deep into the miracle of compounding. In fact, we will see that the reinvestment of dividends in a fully diversified dividend growth stock portfolio, is actually a story of compounding within compounding within compounding—a leveraging of math and time that ought to be irresistible.

Investment advisors have been building financial plans around "systematic withdrawals" from diversified portfolios forever. But what if the assets one is withdrawing from are in an [inevitable] period of decline? How does one withdrawing from their nest egg insulate themselves from the realities of a bear market? One fact changed my thinking forever—stock price appreciation goes positive, and negative; dividend payments can only be positive. Fluctuation in value is part of being an investor, but tapping the source of only positive returns in negative markets goes a long way to preserving your income flow for the long haul.

Perhaps compounding the reinvestment of dividends is a great way to build wealth around stable, healthy companies. And perhaps the withdrawal of a growing flow of positive dividend payments is a defensive way to ensure your cash flow needs are not exposed to bad timing risk. But is the cost of this strategy a significantly lower total return over time? Is the opportunity cost severe? Not only is the Yield on Original Investment something investors must understand, but they may be shocked at the real performance history as well.

The loss of purchasing power is one of the greatest threats investors face, and no shortage of strategies exist as to how to deal with it. But rather than speculate on wildly volatile commodities or metals which offer no internal rate of return, why not look at the most historically verifiable method of defeating inflation we have found? Companies that can increase their prices with the reality of inflation (after all, is there inflation if they are not doing so?), and companies that can (and do) increase the dividend they pay us along the way!

The systemic change in executive compensation over the last twenty to twenty-five years has also led to a systemic change in how companies return cash to shareholders. An analysis of the pros and cons of different ways companies do this, and what it means relative to dividend growth, provides pleasant surprises for investors.

The vast majority of the dividend growth orientation is undermined by companies that cut their dividends. Indeed, many advisors avoid this approach to investing because it cannot be merely indexed by a backward-looking understanding of a company's dividend habits. What goes into the hard work necessary to find sustainable dividend growth in the companies that belong in a quality growth and income portfolio?

The most common mistake people make is believing that "high yielding" stocks are the pot of gold dividend-growth investors are after. But sometimes the surest way to end up with a "no yield" stock is to buy a "high yield" one. The differentiation between high yielders and tomorrow's growers is striking. Free cash flow vs. good intentions is important. And "sectors" are not.

# INTRODUCTION

*"One's destination is never a place, but rather a new way of looking at things."*

—HENRY MILLER

The late 1990s were not merely a profitable time to be investing in stocks—they were exhilarating. The leg of the bull market that lasted from 1995 through early 2000 created annual returns in the S&P 500 that are almost impossible to believe:[1]

| | | |
|---|---|---|
| 1995: +37.58% | 1997: +33.36% | 1999: +21.04% |
| 1996: +22.96% | 1998: +28.58% | |

And these returns in the broad index S&P 500 do not even touch those of the technology-heavy Nasdaq:[2]

| | | |
|---|---|---|
| 1995: +39.92% | 1997: +21.64% | 1999: +85.59% |
| 1996: +22.71% | 1998: +39.63% | |

These average annualized returns of 41.9% for the Nasdaq and 28.7% for the S&P 500 speak to the exuberance of the second half of that decade, but they fail to capture the sociology of the era—the poetry of the moment, if you will. With returns like those, particularly ones so focused in limited sectors (or just one sector!), discussions about traditional concepts like asset allocation, diversification, risk management, fundamental analysis, intrinsic value, and yes, dividend growth, were seemingly obsolete, foreign, unnecessary, laughable, or even contemptible.

Apart from the impact this leg of the bull market had on the way investors approached their portfolios and retirement savings, and apart from the way financial professionals were often moved to become performance-chasing stock jockeys (by their clients as much as any other force!), the society itself reflected the excitement of the era. E*Trade became famous for iconic Super Bowl commercials touting easy access to riches through day-trading in this stock frenzy. Celebrities were hired en masse to serve as spokespeople for different dot-com companies, brokerage firms, or other parts of the era's "supply chain" in new investing. Bars were filled with modestly-paid people talking about the daily gains in their brokerage accounts. IPO became a household acronym. Business models were re-branded to account for the potential of a digital reach, even if that reach was non-existent or, more commonly, a big drag on earnings.

The entire story of 1995–1999 cannot be linked to just dot-com madness and the Nasdaq bubble. The S&P 500 returns reflected growth across other sectors of the economy, all of which were benefitting from not just technological advancements, but the very legitimate economic growth the world was experiencing. Rapid acceleration in globalization had led to entirely new markets, and the 1994 implementation of NAFTA had profound impacts on comparative advantage. New markets meant new revenues, new profits, and new investing opportunities. The business-friendly period of the 1980s had seen taxes and regulations come down from the oppressive levels of the late 1960s and 1970s, and the 1990s were continuing that wave of economic growth. The rapid growth of the 401k industry as a means of providing retirement benefits to workers had created enormous new flows into equity markets. The mutual fund industry exploded as investors large and small sought the convenience of packaged, diversified access to stocks.

It was a bull market built on a solid foundation, but one almost sure to end in excess.

The problem with identifying excess is timing its date of fruition. Former Federal Reserve chair Alan Greenspan famously noted his concern about "irrational exuberance" in late 1995. The bull market would grow leaps and bounds for four more years, and then some, before "irrational exuberance" would be called "irrational" again.

Greed is a powerful motivator. So is pride. Investors were not just afraid of losing the profits that might be had if they failed to purchase [fill in the blank].com stocks during this period; they were afraid of missing a chance to thump their chest in glory at such gains. The profit motive was key but so was the social strata motive—the opportunity for those playing this game of big bragging rights at the gym, the lunch room, and the weekend clubs. No one was getting attention boasting about style-box investing[3] or buying dividend value names, even as returns in the more traditional and fundamental aspects of investing markets were quite good. The large-cap value index (Russell 1000 Value) was still up 23.6% annually over this five-year period, and the small-cap index (Russell 2000) was up 17.2% annually itself.[4] But those returns were not sufficient for the era—and don't even get me started on bonds! An investment in the ten-year Treasury bond would have created an annual return of 8.3% over this five-year period,[5] unacceptable for so many with stocks in the stratosphere.

By now, you may be in a state of shock to think about the idea of 24% returns in value stocks and 8% in bonds being considered "sub-par," but that is because we have been back in reality for a long time now, and the era of the late 1990s was not reality. In fact, it proved to be the preface to what was an unfathomably bad decade for risk asset investors: the first decade of the 2000s.

Equity markets entered the year 2000 the way they ended 1999: on a tear. The dreaded Y2K fear proved to be the sham many of us forecasted it would be, and markets worked off that drag in short order. The Federal Reserve had been letting the good times roll, the world of new tech felt like a world of new investment returns, and global economic conditions were favorable. The Cold War had been over for a decade, developing countries were seeing the creation of a middle class en masse, and peace was the primary state of much of the globe.

And then March 2000 happened. (See Figure I–1.)

In reality, the famous month was not particularly noteworthy for the Dow Jones Industrial Average or the S&P 500. The S&P 500 was actually up in March, though it declined a modest 5% in the two months that followed. But the Nasdaq began a drop that would reach 34% in just one calendar month. The violence would continue throughout 2000, 2001, and 2002, with returns of -39.2%, -21%, and -31.5% (in a row), welcoming the boom investments of the prior decade to the bust environment of the new millennium.[6]

Perhaps investors could have shrugged off the slaughter in the technology sector. No doubt, it hurt many investors and caught many off guard, but many knew by 2000 that they had been riding one unprecedented wave, and surely some profits had been earned along the way. The sudden violence of the initial sell-off in the Nasdaq surely gave many investors the chance to take their lumps and leave the high-flying, tech-heavy sector to park in the more modest land of the S&P 500.

But alas, the spillover carnage from the technology sector had already impacted the S&P 500. The S&P 500 itself had become 35% weighted in technology by the height of the market bubble, more than double its now thirty-year track record of 16%.[7]

The S&P is a market-cap weighted index, meaning that the weight of each constituent automatically grows in the index as its market capitalizations (i.e. stock prices) grow. The technology boom was not just bringing the overall price level of the S&P 500

**FIGURE I–1**

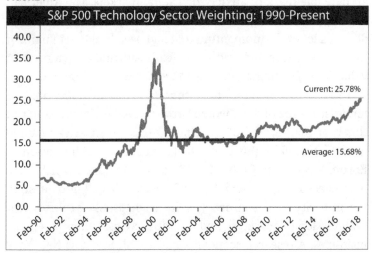

S&P 500 Technology Sector Weighting: 1990-Present

Current: 25.78%

Average: 15.68%

Source: Bespoke's S&P 500 Sector Weightings Report, 2018

higher, but it was increasing the percentage of technology exposure within the index higher as well.

The S&P 500 closed the year 2000 down by over 9%: a rough year but hardly the worst. The drop was attributed almost entirely to its technology holdings: the S&P Technology sector dropped 29% on the year, as did the closely related S&P Telecom sector. But the 35% gain in financials, 47% gain in health care, and 29% gain in energy[8] all created a useful offset to the index's technology pain for the first year of the bear market that was to come.

The year 2001 became a different story, for a whole different reason. While the economy worked to shake off the effects of the technology sector bust, the worldwide expansion of emerging markets was creating incredible opportunities in the materials and consumer sectors. But on September 11, 2001, disaster struck the United States of America. The unprecedented terror attacks on American soil not only took three thousand lives, but they left an indelible mark of anxiety on capital markets. The American economy and her capital markets would recover, as they always do, but a lot of the momentum that had been building in parts of the economy reversed, and a new fear headwind overcame asset valuations. The market dropped 12% for the calendar year.

Shockingly, neither the technology bust of 2000 nor the terrorist horror of 2001 would prove to be the worst chapter of this bear market. In 2002, faith and trust in American capital markets would be put through the ringer as the implosion of Enron, WorldCom, Global Crossing, and Adelphia, which were behind accounting scandals and fraud, would call into question the integrity of the entire system. High profile bankruptcies, Congressional hearings, and criminal arrests dominated the headlines. A research scandal plagued Wall Street as New York lawmakers extracted fines from the big financial firms for alleged conflicts of interest between their research and investment banking departments. Insider trading scandals (and arrests) made the news. And as these headline events continued, the U.S. economy itself entered a mild recession. The market would drop over 22% for the year 2002, which when compounded with its two prior years, amounted to a 38% decline over three calendar years—what we refer to as a "peak-to-trough" decline. Welcome to the new millennium!

As the U.S. economy is prone to do, there was a significant recovery from what ailed it in the first few years of the 2000s. Just as the hallowed grounds of Ground Zero were cleaned up, so the dust settled in capital markets, and normalcy began to return to markets in late 2002 and early 2003. Excessively easy monetary policy helped fuel a recovered appetite for risk assets, and not even a war with Iraq was able to stop the economy and the market from meaningfully advancing from 2003 to 2006.

Unfortunately, too much of the recovery proved to be the result of an expanding credit bubble that was destined to not end well. A housing bubble, forming for years, accelerated to a level never thought possible, and the extraction of equity from the housing sector fueled a consumer spending binge. Market interest rates were historically low, driving capital in a search for yield. A perfect storm had gathered for an unprecedented credit and housing bubble to explode. And explode it did. First, the subprime credit market blew up in August 2007, and significant questions surfaced about how severe the contagion effect would prove to be. From there, the news would be one disastrous event after another throughout 2007 and the first half of 2008 (the collapse of New Century Financial, the collapse of Countrywide, the stunning demise of Bear Stearns and its rescue by JP Morgan). But nothing would prepare markets, or the world, for what was to come in September 2008.

The Treasury Department exercised the legal authority it had secured from Congress that summer to take custody of Fannie Mae and Freddie Mac. Housing prices had continued to drop, and access to credit markets was nearly impossible to come by. Financial institutions did not trust each other's marks—what they were claiming about the value of assets on their books—and for good reason. Firms that relied on short-term borrowing to fund their operations were in danger of losing access to the liquidity they needed to survive.

This came to a head with one particularly over-leveraged Wall Street firm, Lehman Brothers, on September 15, 2008. The legendary firm desperately tried to secure a government bailout or a private rescuer, but failed in both. Their bankruptcy announcement brought the world's capital markets to their knees. Money market funds dried up. Merrill Lynch was forced into a desperate sale to Bank of America. Morgan Stanley was forced into a desperate partial sale to Mitsubishi. Wachovia fell to Wells Fargo. Washington Mutual to JP Morgan. Goldman Sachs secured capital from Warren Buffett. And AIG was forced into the hands of the United States government, now serving as the insurer for many of the Wall Street firms needing to cash in on the insurance.

The collapse was nowhere near limited to the carnage in financial stocks. Real GDP contracted by 4.2% over the eighteen-month recession, the worst contraction in the U.S. economy since the Great Depression. Nearly nine million jobs were lost.[9] And housing prices entered utter free fall. Foreclosures skyrocketed. The period saw 2.5 million businesses close.[10] There was no aspect of the economy not feeling the pain. From the market peak in October 2007 to its bottom in March 2009, the S&P 500 declined a stunning 56.4%. The calendar year return for just 2008 was down 37%.

In early March 2009, markets began their inevitable recovery. The economy had not yet begun to turn up, unemployment would not find its peak for well over a year, and GDP growth remained negative. But markets began to improve because they were just tired of going down. A suspension of mark-to-market accounting helped. The Federal Reserve's aggressive interventions (0% fed funds rate and the beginning of quantitative easing) helped. But nothing helped more than the violence and severity of the decline itself. Markets began to go up because they had gone down enough.

What I describe in the preceding pages—the dramatic, severe market extremes, the most surreal of booms and busts— all took place within *one measly calendar decade*. The market has seen bubbles and booms before. The S&P had been impacted by corporate scandals, geopolitical threats, and mild recessions before—but not all three at once. Markets have seen multi-year bull markets since the beginning of markets, but the up and down movements of 1998–2008 were not ordinary up and down movements. (See Figure I–2.)

**FIGURE I–2**

This was also my first decade as an investor and investment professional—marked by a massive bull run, followed by a terrible bear sell-off, followed by another bull run, followed by the mother of all sell-offs, and in the end a completely lost decade for those seeking equity market returns.

Two things must be said: (1) Since the point where the chart above leaves off in 2008, the markets have advanced over 300%. New highs were long ago made, overcoming the downturn of the financial crisis and rewarding many times over the investors who stayed faithful to the equities despite the collapse of 2008. And, (2) This was not a normal decade. Rolling ten-year periods like this have happened but are hyper-rare. For quite a few reasons, no perspective says that that particular decade is likely to repeat itself, in the same way, again.

That initial decade in my investing life is not some cloud that follows me as I make decisions about the next year, or five years, or decade. Indeed, despite my complete confidence in the inevitability of disruption and distress in capital markets every so often, I strongly suspect that decade will be the worst one I encounter as a financial professional (though I surely wouldn't guarantee it!).

That decade did not cause me to treat certain events as normative that shouldn't be, and it did not cause me to assume the worst about capital markets for future retiree clients. But it did cause me to embark on a much fuller intellectual adventure to rethink everything I had believed about investing. The reality of the financial crisis had a profound impact on my beliefs about the role of behavioral management in an investor's financial outcomes (hint: I believe it is basically everything that matters).

I believed well before the financial crisis—and believe to this day—that the opportunity for regular investors to participate in the future earnings growth of the world's greatest companies is, indeed, the best opportunity for passive wealth creation ever invented.[11] This belief stems from my belief that free enterprise—the engine of innovation and growth unleashed by mankind's search for a better life—is permanently investible. There is no capitalism without capital markets and when I invest in the great equity markets that fuel modern capitalism, I am a co-participant in an extraordinary engine of wealth creation.

I believe economics to be the study of human action; I believe human action seeks incentives and results that advance its quality of life. Profits get made in that pursuit and the incentives of profit drive those very pursuits further. Public equity markets are an opportunity for me to participate in this engine, and they do so with easy access for entrance, easy ability to exit, phenomenal efficiency, and even reasonably benign tax consequences.

When it comes to investing client capital (which at press time, I and my co-laborers at The Bahnsen Group do on behalf of over $1.5 billion of such capital) I recognize that the engines of free enterprise must be monetized in the context of individual needs: individual appetites for volatility, specific liquidity profiles, individual tax ramifications, and the timelines specific to each investor's objectives.

My broad passion for capital markets as a corollary to my passion for free enterprise was made more specific after the financial crisis. While rising stock prices and rising market multiples may very well create an index return that meets my clients' goals, the fact of the matter is that my passion is for real companies creating real products and real services and, from that effort, generating real profits. The accounting scandals at the beginning of the millennium reinforced that a company can be very "profitable" even as they are bleeding cash. Indeed, the value destruction inside the great financial firms of Wall Street reinforces this even more. This caused me to appreciate the concept of "free cash flow," something we will address much more throughout this book.

I came to the realization that investors do not take on the risk of capital markets merely for the *theoretical* gain of profits and a system of innovation, enterprise, and all the rest; they engage in the investment activity for the *actual* gain. Innovative companies serving their customers, making new markets, and creating value generate profits that result in excess cash flow, and investors can monetize their investments when a portion of that cash flow is returned to them in the form of dividends.

As I was in the midst of this intellectual journey, a good friend, Luke Theeuwes, introduced me to the work of Lowell Miller and the asset management firm of Miller/Howard Investments. I became deeply influenced by the same discoveries that had so profoundly impacted Lowell Miller's beliefs about equity investing. As long as cash flows are growing year over year, why shouldn't the dividends we receive be growing year over year? And couldn't an investor in the withdrawal phase of her financial life insulate herself from the risk of withdrawing from a ten-year flat market by focusing on these dividends? And for that investor just building and accumulating wealth for the future, couldn't they reinvest these dividends to create a compounding machine of future income?

In this book, I do not suggest that what we will call dividend growth investing is the *only* sensible way for an investor to invest. Nor do I intend to suggest it is the "best" way—defining "best" is too subjective, and too silly. I do suggest that it is the *right* way for me to invest, for it meets the core of what I believe about investing:

It is fundamental, not superstitious.

It is rooted in reality, not speculation.

It is thoughtful, not faddish.

It is time-tested, not novel.

It does not require a "flavor of the month" approach, and it does not work for some but fail for others. It is a powerful tool for both withdrawers of capital and accumulators of capital alike.

At my firm, we invest in emerging markets, fixed income, alternatives, real estate, small cap stocks, and numerous other asset classes that we believe play a role in the proper diversification of an individual client portfolio. Dividend growth stocks do not make up 100% of what we do or what we believe in, and we do not advocate this for anyone. But dividend growth stocks are the core building block of our portfolios—customized in weighting and allocation for each individual client—for all the reasons I will now present in this book, making the case for dividend growth investing as:

- ▶ The ultimate optimization of what investing is supposed to be.
- ▶ A necessary part of the history of stock market returns.
- ▶ A pivotal way to learn about the company you are investing in from the perspective of those who actually run it.
- ▶ A way of creating a literal miracle of compounding in your portfolio, layered by more compounding miracles.
- ▶ A way of insulating an investor from the dangers of withdrawing capital during periods of extended market distress (like the decade this introductory chapter walked through).
- ▶ A means of pursuing superior risk-adjusted returns, not inferior ones, as many wrongly believe.
- ▶ A protection against the insidious effects of inflation on long-term purchasing power.
- ▶ A superior tool for companies to return cash to shareholders vs. stock buybacks.
- ▶ A strategy that requires active engagement, lest the great evil of dividend cuts sneak up while not paying attention.
- ▶ A bottom-up investment strategy rooted in great companies with great free cash flow (not accidental high yielders).

Through it all, I hope you will at least be informed by the perspective that guides my own investment worldview. I do not strive to persuade you of anything, but I do hope to demonstrate for you this practical message that has become such a huge part of my life and career:

*Financial goals are real, and their outcomes will be real, too, one way or the other. The investment strategies that support their success ought to be real as well. Dividend growth stocks get to the heart of what is real in investing.*

# 1

## WHY PEOPLE INVEST
### Cash Flow is King

*"I am more concerned with the return of my money than the return on my money."*

—WILL ROGERS

I have had several epiphanies in my career as a portfolio manager. Some are ones I should have had much earlier than I did. Some were epiphanies to me, but nothing new to many people much smarter than I. And some were transformative events in my life, career, and entire approach to serving my clients. What I write about in this chapter falls into that category.

But before I unpack the epiphany I am describing, it might help for me to cover some of the things I am *not* referring to— but foundational facts and principles that govern so much of my investment worldview, and ought to govern yours, too, even if these things did not come to me as a transformative epiphany.

### Human Nature Decides All

I believe a lot more about investing than what the subject of this book covers. More importantly, I believe a lot more about how a person's financial goals are met than what is embedded in a

1

philosophy of dividend growth. Truth be told, I believe that an investor can agree intellectually with every word I write in this book—the idea that cash flow-generative investments with the ability and likelihood to grow their income year-over-year make for a dependable growth, income, and growth-of-income strategy—and yet completely fail in their financial goals.

I actually don't really believe *the strategy* will fail, and I don't believe the risk/reward trade-off I will write about will fail to achieve its desired aim. **But at the cornerstone of my convictions about wealth management is that one's temperament trumps their intellect, one's emotions supersede their agreements, and that human nature is the force which must be contended with above all others.** Yes, I engage the challenges of markets each and every day. Yes, designing an optimal asset allocation and constructing a productive portfolio is a daunting task. But the value-added to the lives of investors who are kept from surrendering to their worst instincts is a value that surpasses all other services and work.

Our industry often calls it "behavioral modification," and that term is fine as far as it goes. But what I am describing is more than just the needed hand-holding when one is considering a panic portfolio exit when the markets are dropping. It is more than just talking down the forces of greed when one is presented with some hair-brained "easy money" idea. It involves an entire framework for the relationships we have with our clients—one that is constantly aware of the pull that psychology and emotion represent; one that seeks from the outset to respect the potency of those forces by not exposing clients to a pain or trauma which will force them into a decision they lack the will to resist.

## Given Human Nature, Trust is Imperative

It should be said, the framework of which I speak also recognizes that being aware of these "tension points" and "breaking points" is not possible in any quantifiable or formulaic kind of way ("Dear Mr. Client, our studies show that you have a tolerance of 20% downside, but we are only down 19.5%, so you should be fine"). Rather, it is the burden, the *aim*, of the relationship to be constantly instilling the faith, confidence, and comfort needed so that Mr. or Ms. Client might be as armed as possible against the behavioral forces of financial catastrophe.

The concept I am describing is one of *trust*. Investors are paying us, in some measure, to help guide them around human nature's efforts to distort their financial objectives. Our ability to do this is entirely based on that client's ability to trust us. And their ability to trust us is entirely based on our *trustworthiness*. It is a virtuous cycle, if there ever was one.

We do not believe we earn the trust of clients if we lie to them. We believe that what we present to clients and what we do on their behalf must be rooted in truth, or reality. If we tell a client that there is a high-flying momentum growth stock that is going to keep going up, and that we will have them out just before it collapses, we may very well prove accidentally right. But we did not tell them the truth. We got lucky. Speculation may be a perfectly legitimate part of an investor's portfolio, especially if defined as such in their investment objectives and quantified as a reasonable part of their risk capital in their financial planning and assessment. But presenting speculation as something other than speculation is never appropriate. Our goal is to invest client capital, and our own, in a way that reinforces trust. For no matter how good or bad one's approach to capital markets may be, if the investing client loses trust in the person or people implementing that approach, poor behavioral decisions will undo all the good of that given portfolio approach.

Our commitment to truth-telling, to trustworthiness, to behavioral guidance as our key value proposition, and to divi-dend growth investing, are not separated from one another. We believe they are all profoundly and intimately connected, and serve as vital pieces of the same puzzle in achieving financial goals for clients.

## A Coherent Plan Must Guide the Portfolio

Besides my commitment to a foundation of trust in our relationships with clients, I also believe that a coherent and thorough plan must guide the portfolio. This was not a real epiphany; I have known it and tried my best to implement it since my career began. Because I studied economics long before I studied portfolio management, I already knew that "money" is better defined as "purchasing power." It is intuitively true that our work on behalf of clients must succeed in delivering needed purchasing power, as opposed to a random and not properly understood absolute value. As Chapter 7 will reveal, dividend growth investing is uniquely capable of delivering this objective.

Asset allocation's role in driving an investor outcome was never a real epiphany for me, either. There obviously was some early point where the basic terms and concepts had to be defined and defended for me, but the idea that every investor's portfolio is allocated some way, whether they did it on purpose or not, and that an intentional and strategic approach to designing such a portfolio would be advantageous to the end result, was hardly controversial. The mix of assets to drive a unique risk/reward/liquidity/tax picture is sensible and foundational. And dividend growth investing is perfectly compatible with such thinking.

## Volatility is Inevitable

I also never expected for my clients' portfolios to achieve the results they needed without any form of volatility. The idea of promising volatility-free returns not only strikes me as a profound violation of my earlier commitment to trustworthiness, but also violates the inviolable fact of risk premium. That is, that the return in excess of the risk-free rate represents an investor's compensation for the volatility they incur. Dividend growth investing is not immune from the reality of stock market volatility. It may very well be that for reasons we will unpack in Chapter 3, dividend growth equities often incur less volatility in periods of heightened market distress, but the basic market volatility that is a necessary ingredient of stock market reality is very much alive and well in this space, too.

## The Malady of Perma-Bearism

That perma-bearism is a sociological and psychological malady, not a thoughtful investment worldview, did not come to me as an epiphany. My success in unpacking where perma-bears came from was enhanced through more experience and more exposure, but early on it was clear that realism belonged to the optimists, and that doomsdayism did not come from an outlook one had on capital markets, but rather from one of two things: (1) A crass and exploitive desire to monetize other people's fear (this is highly true of the "no skin in the game" newsletter industry, where writers who have never managed a dollar of real capital in their lives use their fearmongering to generate subscription and advertising revenue); or (2) A sincere but sad view of reality that is conspiratorial, not rooted in history, and driven more by what it wants to happen than what it believes will happen.

There was no epiphany necessary to see that market bears have a desire to sound smart, and have a remarkable ability to take credit when the clock is right twice per day.

## The Insanity of Market Timing

I suppose the insanity of market timing has been reinforced in more intellectually convincing and emotionally satisfying ways over the years, but there was never a time when I really believed that I, or anyone else, could do what the great investors of all time could not do. I freely acknowledge that if one's investment strategy was successfully executed as...

*Being in the market all the times it was up*
AND
*Being out of the market all the times it was down*

...they would have an incredible and unbeatable record to contend with. Indeed, it is hard to imagine a better strategy than having a crystal ball as to when markets will be up vs. down. It is also hard to comprehend why one would ever limit leverage if they possessed such ability. With that said, I will reserve my dripping sarcasm for my weekly www.dividendcafe.com columns, and not let it take over this book.

Suffice it to say, this ability is not held by anyone—not by the greatest of money managers and hedge funds in the world, and not by your CPA, barber, bartender, or uncle.

\* \* \* \* \*

None of these six revelations, principles, or tenets speak to the epiphany—a truly transformational epiphany—that drives the premise of this book.

The epiphany I had many years ago was this:
*All investors invest for a return of cash. Period.*

You can respond to this in one of two ways—by immediately agreeing with how obvious it is, or by fighting it for being so obviously wrong. If your reaction is the former, you probably aren't getting what I mean (for it is not obvious), and if your reaction is the latter, I need to exhaustively elaborate. We'll start there.

Imagine any financial situation you want, with any goals, timeline, criteria, people, and particulars you want. Imagine four or five situations, each with completely different variables, all meant to disprove the idea that investors invest for a return of cash. Let's see where this gets us.

▶ The most obvious example is someone saving for retirement. They are investing now, trying to build a mass of funds that will one day be used to pay them cash flow when their current source of cash flow (employment) goes away. No one would dispute that that investor is looking for future cash from the money he puts into investments today.

▶ Consider a situation where we will not need a future "stream of income" (like a retiree), but a lump sum (saving for an eventual purchase of a boat, a house down payment, a college graduation, a wedding, and so forth). Almost just as easily as the first example, this person is investing for cash that will come back to them in the future.

▶ Institutionally, pensions and endowments are almost as easy as the first two examples. Money is put away today to send out a cash commitment stream later (in the future with a pension, perhaps in the present with an endowment).

▶ Now let's make it harder. What if an investor said, "I do not need the money ever returned to me. I have more than enough income and assets to meet my needs for my entire life. I want to grow this portfolio as much as possible for my grandchildren's future." Notice the key objective. They may not need "cash" in their lifetimes, but the purpose has not changed, just the timeline for the return of cash in the future to their grandchildren (whether as a perpetual stream, or in lump sum).

▶ Harder still? When one says they just want to see their value go higher—they have no income objective—they are not looking to bury the money. It may be for a legacy (family, children), but the investment has no utility to them or anyone or anything they care about unless some day it is monetized. That monetization may come from a sale (asset A was bought for X, and many years later sold for something more than X, perhaps many multiples of X), or it may come from the investment kicking off cash flow (what we call dividends). But in any scenario, the eventual objective is a return of cash, partial or full, on some timeline (short or long).

Once you digest what I am saying, you will at least see the futility of arguing with it. Even legacy investments are not exceptions; even they are expected to create some cash flow along the way or to be monetized for some beneficiary at some point (if one pretends their passion is for their great-great-great grandchildren, it still won't negate what I am getting at).

The bigger question is not whether or not this is true, for in the very basic sense of things, it is indisputably so. The question is what it has to do with anything, and how this epiphany served as an early catalyst in my understanding about dividend growth.

Where people resist the idea of cash flow investing is when they pretend growth and income are separate objectives. As we have already covered, calling someone a "growth" investor may simply be a reference to their timeline, but it is not a claim that they have no interest in the future return of cash. A "current income" objective is easy to identify, and so is a "future income" investment. But I contend that the nomenclature of "growth" vs. "income" is mere semantics, a reference to *mechanics* and possibly a reference to *timeline*, but not at all a separation between "one who doesn't ever want cash" and one who does. Chapters 4 and 5 will unpack what these mechanical issues may mean for an accumulator of capital vs. a spender of capital.

And it should be said—nothing about the epiphany that all investing amounts to a return of cash negates the fact that buying a stock for ten dollars, holding it for a long time, and then one day selling it for a hundred dollars, could very well be the best way to achieve a return of cash. I don't happen to think it is, but for now I am simply trying to establish that buying a stock at one price for the purpose of one day selling it at a higher price is just as much a cash flow-generative strategy (when it works) as buying a stock that pays you a dividend year over year over year. Thought processes may be different, timelines may be different, and certainly risks and mechanics are different, but no, the end goal is not different. In some form or another, people invest for a future cash flow.

Once I realized that the barriers put up in the investing world between "growth" and "income" were possibly artificial, or at least unhelpful, a sort of second epiphany hit me that, when married to this first one, became the foundation of an investing worldview that I believe in with every ounce of breath in my body.

My friends at Miller/Howard Investments refer to this second epiphany as "Yield on Original Investment."[12] It points out that for an investor who is looking to receive cash, the "yield" she cares about is not the "cash divided by current stock price" as much as the "cash divided by original investment." A stock bought at $25, paying $1 in dividends, has a 4% yield at purchase. But if in twenty-five years, when cash back from that investment is needed, the annual dividend is now $21, the investor is actually receiving 85% (per year) in "yield on their original investment." Granted, that stock price is surely much, much higher than $25 if the dividend itself is $21. Indeed, the stock would probably be something like $400 or higher, meaning the "current yield" we spend so much time talking about is only 4–5%.

But what does the investor care about more? In this case, he or she wouldn't have to pick. If they need to go buy a boat, they have a huge gain in capital as their stock appreciated a great deal over twenty-five years. If they need current and recurring income, they can now get 85% of what they invested, in perpetuity, and hold on to the massively appreciated value of the underlying investment. Indeed, if that company has grown their dividend 9% per year for twenty-five years, chances are this company is not done growing their dividend, and it is a part of the ethos of the organization (see Chapter 3). So now the investor has an annual cash flow practically equal to what they paid for the stock twenty-five years earlier.

What were the inputs used to create this hypothetical? You will note, I made no prediction or forecast about the stock price whatsoever in formulating its future dividend payout. In fact, I loosely did the opposite—I estimated that *if* the annual dividend (hypothetically) were $21 in twenty-five years, the former $25 stock price would probably be somewhere around $400 in the future. I was valuing the future stock price (which I can't know) around the future dividend. And how did I get to a future dividend of $21 in twenty-five years, from $1 today? I simply took a 4% yield ($1 dividend on $25 stock price), and had that dividend grow 9% per year for twenty-five years, being reinvested along the way.[13] That *math* gets to a $21 dividend in twenty-five years.

Is a company guaranteed to grow their dividend 9% per year? Of course not. Are there other factors that have to be evaluated in this exercise, especially when contextualized for an investor's real life? Certainly.

But I will argue in this book that finding companies that right now have a 2.5%, or 3.5%, or 5% yield (which we believe may grow their dividends 8%, 9%, 10%, or higher for the next couple decades), is a far less speculative strategy than picking stocks that you think will go up 1,600% in the next twenty-five years. Indeed, I will argue that the likelihood of staying in a stock long enough to make that kind of return is far easier with a continually growing dividend than it is without one. And I will argue that the compounding of the dividend along the way is actually the greatest contributor to that company's total return over that period.

Are there stocks that will go up 1,600% with no dividend, in a shorter period of time? Sure there are. Will you own them? Maybe you will own one. Maybe more. But what are the odds that you will get that kind of return from pure capital appreciation, with no dividend to help, and without other stocks in that hot pursuit blowing up on you along the way?

My epiphanies did not replace the math of high growth stock appreciation, but it did force a rather revelatory internal conversation about risk, reward, and reality.

And it forced me into a deep analysis of history. I found company after company with a 2% or 3% or 4% yield *now*, where the annual cash payment was actually 50%, 75%, 100%, or higher of the original cost of that same investment!

Consider the following companies, just to see what their stock prices were the year I was born (1974), what their dividends were then, what those yields were at that time, what the dividends are now, and what that "YOI" (yield on original investment) is today in Figure 1–1:[14]

**FIGURE 1–1**

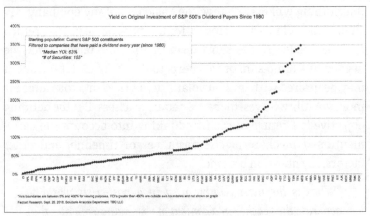

There is a self-fulfilling prophecy in the stock prices of these companies. Many would say, "that's great that you have such a high YOI, but who cares if you have such a great gain in the stock price!" This logic forgets several key things, often forgotten outside the world of dividend growth:

1. Investment gains come from the belief of future profits, or they come from real profits;
2. If, from real profits generously shared with shareholders, investors have a chance to compound their gains through reinvestment of dividends (see chapter 4), and
3. Along the way in obtaining this great performance, the dividend told us something about the company that we would not have known without it or, better put, management used the dividend to tell us something we would not have otherwise known. (see chapter 3)

Third-party marketers, institutional consultants, and all sorts of layered bureaucrats in the supply chain of asset management have a good reason to like terms such as "growth" vs. "value" and "moderate" vs. "conservative." There are good and bad reasons to put labels on different aspects of one's portfolio. But nothing will ever change the basic fact of my epiphany: My clients, like all investors, invest for a return of cash. That return may be needed in the short term or the long term, it may be needed in a lump sum or in a perpetual state of cash flow, and it may be desired with limited volatility in prices or a tolerance for more volatility. So yes, there are details to assess. But the defining objective is a return of cash, and taking into account the aforementioned mechanical circumstances of timeline, and other factors, my question became:

*"What is the most reliable way in a post-crisis world to generate that cash—in a context of risk management—that*

*will enable a high yield some day on the capital one puts to work now?"*

This is to say, how do I find a high Yield on Original Investment for my clients?

These epiphanies created the questions; dividend growth investing became the answer.

# 2

# WHAT'S OLD IS NEW AGAIN

## Historical Context and Realities
## in Dividend Growth

*"I will not abandon a previous approach whose logic I understand even though it may mean foregoing large, and apparently easy, profits to embrace an approach which I don't fully understand, have not practiced successfully, and which could, quite possibly, lead to a substantial permanent loss of capital."*

—WARREN BUFFETT, ANNUAL LETTER, 1967

Raise your hand if you have ever heard this statistic: *The S&P 500 has increased 9.8% for the last ninety years.*

Perhaps you have even seen this chart (Figure 2–1),[15] or some other chart like it, pointing to the reality of a multi-decade advancement in the broad stock market that starts down and to the left, and goes up and to the right:

If you are expecting me to tell you that the data point is wrong or that the chart is misleading, I am afraid you will be disappointed. The fact of the matter is that the S&P 500 has generated that kind of annual return (taken as the average of annual returns), and the chart really does look like that. Granted, inflation has eroded the purchasing power that would come from the

**FIGURE 2–1**

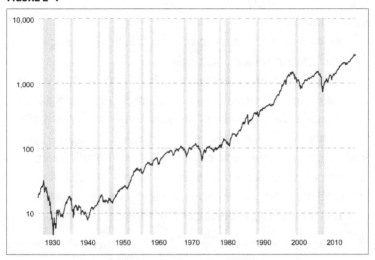

returns a broad-market index like this has generated; that argues all the more for the superior returns asset classes like stocks have generated. And yes, the bear markets that existed within this period of time were brutal when living through them (1974, 1982, 2002, and 2008 particularly come to mind). But the fact of the matter is that a broad-based U.S. equity investor has achieved a nominal pre-tax return of nearly 10 percent per year for almost one hundred years. I share this not only as historical fact; I even suggest that the nature of free enterprise, the profit motive, capital markets, innovation, and the global demand for both risk premium and liquidity all suggest we are very likely to enjoy a wonderful broad market return for many, many decades to come.

Capital's relentless pursuit for its own most efficient allocation is not dead, and neither is free enterprise. I am an equity market bull, meaning that relative to other allocation choices, capturing a claim on the future earnings of the best-run companies is likely to be a highly attractive option for investors for the fore-seeable future.

So what does this have to do with this book's argument for dividend growth equity investing?

A significant amount of what we believe about the historical returns of stocks (believe, because it is true) comes from a period when the dividends investors received were roughly half of the total returns. If that ratio were to be maintained into the future, with a current yield between 1.7% and 2%, it would seemingly indicate a total return in the S&P 500 of roughly 3.5 to 4%—less than half of the return we just got done historically appreciating.

Two things need to be immediately said:

1. In no way am I suggesting that the forward returns of the S&P 500 will now equal something as low as 3.5% or so, and...
2. I do believe that with a dividend yield of the S&P 500 this low, it is important to think differently about growth, income, risk, reward, and the future.

This chapter will seek to unpack all of this, and generate application to contemporary investors.

Total return equals the combination of price apprecia-tion and income received (i.e., dividends). If an investment has returned 10%, and 4% came from dividends, then 6% came from price appreciation. Therefore, if the dividend contribution were to now be +2%, to achieve the same 10% total return, price appre-ciation would need to move from +6% to +8%. To play this out further, this would require a 33% higher return from price appre-ciation than has historically been the case.

Most people reading this would assume a 33% increase in price appreciation over the last "bull market century" is absurd, and immediately become ready to buy whatever argument I am about to make. But there is a vulnerability to the argument I am making. In theory, it is entirely possible that the price appreciation contribution to total return may, indeed, grow above historical levels. For many decades, stock buybacks were not a viable option for what companies did with their post-tax cash. We will discuss in Chapter 8 more aspects of dividends vs. stock buybacks, but for our purposes here, the fact remains that some very legitimate aspects of past stock market returns are compositionally different than they are now.

However, regardless of what the future will create in terms of stock market returns, and the composition of those returns between dividends and price appreciation, the past has demonstrated time and time again the defensive and offensive, benefits of dividends.

Note from the Figure 2–2 chart[16] the role dividends have played in rolling ten-year periods, relative to total returns. You will note that in the worst decades for total return (the Great Depression, the first decade of this Millennium, and the 1970s), dividends played an incredibly important defensive role. The delta between the price-return below (blue bar) and the

**FIGURE 2–2**

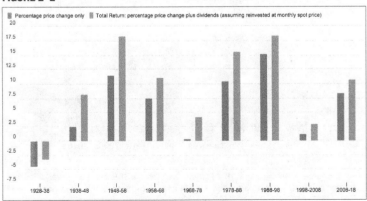

17

total-return (yellow bar) represents the portion of return that has come from dividends. The ability of dividends to soften the negativity of tough markets is indisputable, and cannot be coherently predicted to function differently in the future.

What we know is that since 1930, dividends have represented 42% of the S&P 500's total return (and this is *not* assuming a reinvestment of those dividends!). During robust bull markets like the 1980s and 1990s, that number dropped to 28% and 16%, respectively.[17] Over the last decade, it has represented only 17% of total return. But during the 2000s, it was obviously 100% of the return since there was not a positive total return, and in the 1970s dividends represented 73% of the total return. (Figure 2–3.)

Dividends are a meaningful contribution to total return in any period of time, and an especially meaningful contribution to return when defense is most important to you. Neither one of those statements should be especially controversial. But what about the broader point of source of return, and what the past means about the future?

**FIGURE 2–3**

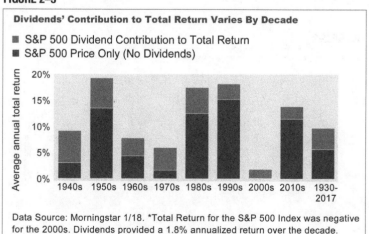

Dividends' Contribution to Total Return Varies By Decade

■ S&P 500 Dividend Contribution to Total Return
■ S&P 500 Price Only (No Dividends)

Data Source: Morningstar 1/18. *Total Return for the S&P 500 Index was negative for the 2000s. Dividends provided a 1.8% annualized return over the decade.

One can say that the future will not look like the past—that the huge contributions dividends meant for the markets from World War Two through the 1980s are a thing of the past—but then why should they say that the past returns of the market are, themselves, relevant? It would seem to me that it is one or the other: it either matters, or it doesn't. But to say that the past matters when discussing historical S&P returns, but does not matter when discussing the composition of said returns, is, well, quite selective.

There is an actual cause-and-effect here, not the mere happenstance of history. During periods of robust, secular expansion (the 1990s come to mind), market valuations were expanding (P/E ratios). Companies were very confident in their ability to re-deploy after-tax profits into company expansion and make investors wait for the monetization of their investment. When business growth seems like it cannot slow down, continued investment into such growth is more likely, hence the lower likelihood for rewarding shareholders with cash during such periods. There is no reason to slam the returns such companies generate during those periods; they have often been robust, hyper-profitable, and impressive.

But of course, that necessarily means that one's exposure to the cyclicality of markets is intensified as well. Historically, the market's greater willingness to reward investors has created a softer backlash during the down periods markets inevitably face. One may say, "I don't want the dividend. Give me more growth and I'll stay leveraged to the secular force driving a company's growth." But saying that means they are disrespecting the very nature of markets. Being bullish on corporate America or free enterprise or on market innovation (all things this author is decidedly bullish on) does not mean being ignorant of business cycles or creative destruction. Years (and decades) gone by where hard-earned company profits were more handsomely paid out to risk-taking shareholders were not periods of inadequate growth, reinvestment, or innovation—quite the contrary! Rather, they were simply periods where the relationship between risk and reward was understood differently.

I would argue that if the opportunity for growth is more intense now than in decades past, it is not an argument for *less dividend payment* but rather more dividend payment! For indeed, it cannot be true in a creatively destructive capitalistic society that only "our company" has the opportunity to reinvest its profits in yet more and more growth. What is sauce for the goose is sauce for the gander, and while "our company" may be laser-focused on such growth, so are the competitors. In other words, the risk is intensified because the opportunity goes higher, not the opposite! All the more reason companies should respect shareholders by rewarding their risk with a share of profits along the way.

The need to balance reinvestment into company growth and fortitude versus rewarding shareholders is not a new or unique discussion. Our American economy seemed to manage a pretty massive amount of growth over many post-war decades, all the while paying out generous dividends to shareholders. That equilibrium between reinvestment and dividend payout (or other forms of returning cash to shareholders like debt reduction or stock buybacks) has been a constant and dynamic process for decades, and will be for decades. Shareholders ought to embrace this tension, and be aware of the benefits to them when the pendulum has swung not so far away from shareholder cash payments.

The historical realities of markets indicate that dividends have played a very important role in decades past in both periods of struggle and periods of expansion. Dividends presently make up much less than 20% of the historical return of the S&P 500. The idea that stock buybacks and prudently executed reinvestment in business growth will compensate investors (through greater price appreciation) for that lower contribution from dividends is entirely possible, but not without an increase in risk exposure. No matter how one slices it, the defensive posture of equity investing is re-composed when dividends are a lower contribution to returns. This is not to say that dividends will not become a higher percentage of return for index investors, or that the way things are positioned now will not end up paying off. Rather, it is simply to point out with mathematical and historical logic that the trade-off of risk and reward is necessarily altered when one consciously goes about pursuing total return this way.

Ironically, not all historical movement has been against dividends. While dividends were a lower contributor to total return in the 1990s and the post-crisis 2010s, the long-term historical record establishes that nearly half of the total return of equities comes from dividends, not even including the impact of compounding (which we will discuss in Chapter 4).

And allow me to provide a key metric around those robust decades of the 1980s and 1990s, where dividends became a mere 20% contributor to total return. A huge part of price appreciation is, always and forever, multiple expansion. Put differently, a rising P/E ratio drives stock prices higher, irrespective of dividend payments. And what creates perhaps the most significant boost to the stock market's P/E ratio? Declining interest rates. What creates the greatest threat to the market's multiple? Rising interest rates. Ultimately, one need not forecast what interest rates will do over the years and decades to come (they won't be accurate even if they tried) to state that interest rates are not going to drop from 18%+ down to 3% as they have over the last thirty years. The mere math of the present interest rate level means that the same degree of multiple expansion is not possible that the 1980s and 90s created.

Does that mean the same total returns are not possible? Not at all! In fact, I believe they are entirely possible—but I believe that to the extent I believe in growing earnings, not growing multiples! And growing earnings means what? More cash, which has to be deployed. Put differently, an analysis of history and light projection about the future suggests that the very factors which previously created a positive total return environment for stocks with little participation from dividends will look very different in the years ahead!

Rather than believing in a "new normal" of light dividend payments coming from America's great companies, the historical reality points to the opposite. Mature companies reach a point where dividend payments become a necessity to properly reward shareholders, as growth rates of the "high octane" years become unrepeatable into the future. The high growth companies that required high reinvestment in the past (think of the great technology companies from the 1990s like Microsoft, Intel, Cisco, and Qualcomm) evolve to a point of stable, impressive, attractive free cash flow generation and reward shareholders with generous dividends rather than risky expansions that violate their stabilized business model. Has any company proven this more than Apple over the last decade or so? High growth companies that mature to the point of dividend leaders are not examples of failure; they are prototypical examples of success! The technology sector alone is responsible for 27% of the increase in market dividends over the last decade,[18] a far cry from past decades where technology was said to be permanently averse to the notion of dividend payments. (See Figure 2–4.)

At the end of the day, the entire subject drastically understates the contribution of dividends to total return for equity investors, because (so far) we are talking about dividends apart from reinvestment of said dividends. You may be impressed (or surprised) by the 42% that dividends represent throughout history in annual returns for an S&P 500 investor, but the truth of the matter is that the number is well above 80% when one factors in dividend reinvestment over a prolonged period of time.[19]

**FIGURE 2–4**

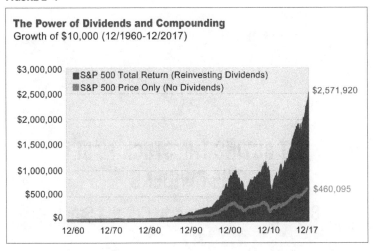

**The Power of Dividends and Compounding**
Growth of $10,000 (12/1960-12/2017)

The role compounding plays in appreciating the upside of dividend growth investing will be the subject of Chapter 4, and will actually transcend the mere historical realities of this chapter. It is when we unpack the mechanics of compounding that we will appreciate the framework of dividend growth as a means of wealth accumulation. For now, though, we simply must understand basic history, which shows us the importance of dividends in an equity investor's total return.

An understanding of markets teaches us that dividends serve as a mitigator of risk, particularly in those periods where risk mitigation proves to be most needed. A dynamic economy means there will be different periods producing different seasons of trend and proclivity around corporate attitude towards dividend payments. And through it all, the resilience of dividends for investors and the resilience of the companies paying them have argued for a dividend-focused investment approach, whether one is looking at risk or reward.

# 3

# NOT BUYING THE STOCK TO GET THE DIVIDEND

## Buying the Dividend to Get the Stock

*"When you combine a culture of discipline with an ethic of entrepreneurship, you get the magical alchemy of great performance."*

—JAMES C. COLLINS

This and the next three chapters will make the financial investment case for dividend growth investing; this is going to be fun. Chapter 4 will dig deep into the mathematical reality of accumulating wealth (and a future flow of income) for those still building their net worth. Chapter 5 is going to make the case for dividend growth for investors in the withdrawal stage of their life. And Chapter 6 is going to defend dividend growth investing for its offense, not merely its defense. There is a different reason to come to the same conclusion about dividend equity investing for accumulators versus withdrawers. These differences are inherently rooted in mechanics, and require the unpacking of the actual dividend itself and how it plays into the process of either accumulating wealth or spending it.

But this chapter will have nothing to do with mechanics. This chapter focuses on the argument for dividend growth investing that I believe most proponents of the approach are, themselves, most likely to miss. The message of Chapter 3 is not at odds with the message of the chapters to come, but rather, complements, facilitates, supplements, and adds to that message. In fact, I will argue that if my only argument for dividend growth investing is the one I will make in this chapter, it alone is sufficient to make the case. I get a chance to quantify the case when we start talking about the compounding of reinvestment. I can validate the protective benefits when I demonstrate the mechanics of withdrawing from positive portfolio cash flow vs. declining asset prices. But at the end of the day, no argument for dividend growth investing is better than the argument of the type of companies actually partaking of the practice themselves!

There is no such thing as a "dividend stock," if one means a particular category companies sign up for when they go public and list their company on an exchange. Sure, there are companies that pay dividends, and companies that do not. There are companies that grow their dividends, and companies that do not. There are companies that used to be dividend payers that no longer are. There are companies that presently pay attractive dividends that used to avoid it altogether. The fact of the matter is that a company is not a dividend stock that then goes out to become a company to serve their customers, to manage their employees, to compete with competitors, to earn a profit. A company has a product or service (or a lot of products and services) that they bring to customers, and do so with effective employee management, competitive superiority, and the achievement of profitability before they are anything. The term "dividend stock" comes later, much later in many cases, as we have seen. Before a company can become a dividend payer, it must first have a business model, a market presence, a means of acquiring customers, a managed cost structure, human capital, development of human talent, systems and processes, and yes, profits. It is that last part—profits—that allow for a conversation about dividends.

Dividends are nothing more than an option of what a company may do with a portion of their profits. Foundational to a company itself is its actual operation, strategy, leadership, employees, sales and marketing, capital structure, and so on. All of these things must be in place before the profits come; in fact, these things are essentially the catalysts to what results in profits. We cannot ever really "buy a dividend" because, whether we think this way or not, what we would be buying is the entity that pays the dividend to us. The dividend is merely the decision of management to pay its shareholders a portion of the profits. It has nothing to do with how the profits were created.

So I would argue that *there is no such thing as a dividend that makes a company great; I would argue that there are merely companies whose dividend points to their greatness.*

Can a company have a defensible business model, an attractive revenue stream, a strong balance sheet, a path to growing earnings, solid competitiveness, best-of-breed talent, and yet pay out no dividend? Of course. And is it possible that a company which checks all those boxes and pays out no dividend is also a solid company, worth investing in, able to generate impressive market returns? Again, of course. It is always *possible.* But when we look at the things we most care about in *companies* we may want to invest in on behalf of our clients, we find time and time again that those characteristics, unrelated to the mechanics of what they do with their after-tax profits, actually happen to occur in dividend payers. There is a virtuous cycle at play between a good company and a robust, growing dividend for shareholders. That virtuous cycle is the story of this chapter.

Modern accounting rules are a thing of beauty. "Generally accepted accounting principles" (GAAP) provide our conventions for financial reporting, and they are surely not rooted in superstition or guesswork. The principles are defensible, rooted in math and science as much as they can be, but more than anything else, they are to be used to tell the story that a company wants reflected from its results. As the *Harvard Business Review* recently said:[20]

> *"In a perfect world, investors, board members, and executives would have full confidence in companies' financial statements. They could rely on the numbers to make intelligent estimates of the magnitude, timing, and uncertainty of future cash flows and to judge whether the resulting estimate of value was fairly represented in the current stock price. And they could make wise decisions about whether to invest in or acquire a company, thus promoting the efficient allocation of capital.*
>
> *Unfortunately, that's not what happens in the real world, for several reasons. First, corporate financial statements necessarily depend on estimates and judgment calls that can be widely off the mark, even when made in good faith. Second, standard financial metrics intended to enable comparisons between companies may not be the most accurate way to judge the value of any particular company—this is especially the case for innovative firms in fast-moving economies—giving rise to unofficial measures that come with their own problems. Finally, managers and executives routinely encounter strong incentives to deliberately inject error into financial statements."*

This is not to say that company financial statements are a mess or even that there is a system better than GAAP to regulate reporting. Pointing out that financial statements can be "gamed" is no more profound than saying anything else about human nature. There are structural issues that just need to be understood, such as:

- ► There is no internationally accepted standard of accounting and financial reporting. The European Union uses what is called the International Financial Reporting Standards (IFRS), while the U.S. uses the aforementioned GAAP. But a huge preponderance of domestic companies have a multi-national presence, often involving actual acquisitions of foreign companies. The way the two accounting measures change how earnings are calculated can be sizable and, in this highly globalized economy, are frequently relevant.

- ► The use of swaps and derivatives can have virtually zero "net impact" for a company's bottom line, and yet can be used (depending on reporting) to substantially change a given optic (top-line revenue, for example).

- ► By definition, "EBITDA" is structurally challenging. It is said to be the "earnings before interest, taxes, depreciation, and amortization expense," but what if that "bad stuff" matters?

Financial statements contain all sorts of information that is extremely important for a financial analyst to assess the outlook for a given company, but they also contain a lot of other information that is not particularly useful (and may, in fact, be dilutive or confusing). The average 10-K report that publicly-traded companies are required to file annually is now well over forty thousand words; often they can exceed a hundred thousand words. My point is not that less disclosures are needed, or that modern accounting does not play a needed role. Rather, the point is that more disclosures can sometimes have the opposite desired effect. And to be somewhat more forceful, talented and creative finance departments can use the financial reports to create selective emphases which may be a distraction to one's investment objective.

What does this have to do with dividend payments? Simply put, dividends are paid with real cash. For all the accounting shenanigans that exist (whether sinister or innocent), real cash is the least likely thing with which to play fast and loose. A company paying out a dividend is making a powerful *accounting statement*, all the more powerful when growing the amount of that dividend. They are saying that they believe in the prospects for the company's growth and strategy, and that they will demonstrate that belief with real cash, which cannot be faked!

I am fond of saying that I assume many people make more money than their "adjusted gross income" (line 37 of the 1040 tax form) says they make. For a variety of reasons, generally driven by the desire to limit tax liability, some people who have the ability to do so very likely seek to minimize the line 37 reading (via understatement of K1 income or 1099 income or schedule "C" income, or the over-utilization of deductions and write-offs). The lower the reported income, the lower the tax liability. However, no one really has incentive to *overstate* their taxable income on their tax return. A guy may say one thing about his earnings power to impress at the bar, but that motivation and corresponding behavior changes quite quickly on one's tax return. No one wants to pay taxes on money they didn't actually earn.

That same principle applies regarding the signal of the dividend. A CEO or CFO saying on a quarterly analyst call, "we really like how we are doing, and not only are proud of our profits last quarter but really confident in the profit growth for next quarter as well," means something, and may very well excite you. However, a CEO or CFO saying on a quarterly analyst call, "we achieved wonderful profits last quarter, and see these profits continuing to grow next quarter and beyond; for that reason, we are increasing the shareholder dividend from [X] to [something more than X]," would really pack quite a different punch, would it not?

The dividend is by no means a sufficient metric for validating a company's financial health, but is it not as powerful and clear and legitimate and real as any other metric (including many other metrics put together)? This entire subject transcends the debate between technicals and fundamentals; it goes to the heart of what we can know and believe about fundamentals to begin with.

Many financial professionals believe in adjudicating a stock's worthiness around "technical analysis;" that is, what it looks like on a chart. In this school of thought, chart patterns and various statistical indicators (backward-looking, by definition) provide great color as to what future stock price movements may be. Complex versions of technical analysis invite an understanding of moving averages and other volume indicators, often interwoven with patterns of prices on a chart. This school of thought is rather severely disinterested in a stock's dividend, and all other fundamentals, for that matter.

The rival school of thought, one this author dogmatically supports, is the school of fundamental analysis. For those interested in fundamentals, the actual performance of the company is what drives stock prices. Valuations matter. Strategy matters. Competitive strength matters. Cash flows matter. Earnings matter. The balance sheet matters. At the end of the day, fundamental analysis seeks to compare the financial outlook of a company to its stock price, and determine if an attractive investment thesis exists. Of course, understanding the fundamentals is easier said than done. Applying one's conclusions about the fundamentals is fallible. The fundamentals can change. This is not a deal-breaker for an investor in risk assets; indeed, it is why investing involves risk. I would just gently suggest that one's investment decisions contain more fallibility when they are divorced from any attempt at cogent analysis. Prudence does not guarantee an accurate result, but it improves the odds.

Where does the dividend fit into the world of fundamental analysis? At the end of the day, the dividend can serve as a reinforcement or validation of the analysis one has done, let alone the analysis or guidance the company itself has provided. The company may have different metrics and valuations around its price relative to its earnings, its sales, or its book value, but the dividend gives us a real-life valuation metric to utilize—one that has "skin in the game" because it forces a company to release cash in making its declaration. Marking company assets at a certain value helps to determine the price-to-book value, but certainly invites subjectivity, fallibility, volatility, and more, to the "fundamental" process. And it does so with little risk to the company, its management, and its financial operations. A dividend, on the other hand, is real-life cash that has left the company bank account in real life when paid out to a real-life shareholder. The money is gone and is not coming back; it will not be a part of the financial operations of the company any more. Like the individual declaring to the Internal Revenue Source the income that he will pay taxes on, this payment has teeth. It has skin in the game.

The verifiability of a company's earnings, and the sustainability of the company's earnings, are not made infallible by the payment of a dividend. Indeed, many companies have used their dividend in the past to try and fool analysts about the health of the business. But when does a company generally admit it is having trouble and cut the dividend: in the ninth inning of its problems, or the first, second, or third inning of its trouble? Any company that continues paying a dividend through nine full innings of trouble is pathologically broken. Chapter 9 will exhaustively address the subject of dividend cuts, and the paramount priority of a dividend growth equity manager to avoid such cuts. Our point here is that in the risky, fallible world of financial projections, one reduces risk and fallibility when real life cash is involved, as it is with dividend payments, particularly dividends that are perpetually growing.

It stands to reason that if a company is growing the dividend they pay shareholders at a pace faster than the earnings themselves are growing, eventually that company will run out of money. The dividends being paid out must be increased at a rate lower than or in line with the earnings growth itself, lest the dividends eventually surpass the earnings and the company be in a negative cash flow. A reliable, sustainable dividend grower therefore must be a reliable, sustainable earnings grower, or the company breaks. The very stability of the dividend growth is an indicator of the reliability of the earnings growth. In short, the reliability of the expectation is enhanced. The dividend growth is pointing both to the more stable company fundamentals, and simultaneously creating more investment stability for the investor. A virtuous cycle, indeed.

What can go wrong here? Well, a lot can. And it is why a prudent advocate for dividend growth equity investing cannot treat all dividend stocks like they are the same. Companies that play financial arbitrage games by borrowing money at a low rate and paying it out in the form of dividend are, in fact, outside the realm of the dividend growth companies I am talking about. The balance sheet of a company indicates its indebtedness, its ratio of debt-to-assets, the nature of the debt it has, and the liquidity of its assets. More importantly, the income statement tells us what kind of income the company is actually earning, and what the use of cash looks like. It is the ability to identify dividends being paid from free cash flow as opposed to dividends being paid from some other source of cash (borrowed funds, retained earnings, or balance sheet capital.) that separates the contenders from the pretenders in dividend growth investing.

In short, a healthy company has manageable debt and solid balance sheet strength. A healthy company has growing free cash flow, and a prudent process for determining what will be needed from its free cash flow to fund capital expenditures, mergers and acquisitions, and other such corporate priorities. A healthy company will have a prudent and generous procedure for determining the dividends available to be paid out from such free cash flow. The prudence and shareholder alignment of such a dividend policy avoids many (most?) corporate financial mistakes, and the ability of the company to have a prudent discipline policy comes from the ability of the company to begin with to sustain a healthy balance sheet and generate defensible and repeatable free cash flow.

These processes do not function independently of each other. They feed on each other. This is a textbook "positive feedback loop" and it is entirely achievable in the world of dividend growth investing.

The vast majority of significant investor losses come from companies that fail to execute a given strategy, and have financial consequences from such failed execution. Excessive debt can be forgiven when a company is executing and servicing the debt; but excessive debt can kill a company when the servicing of said debt exceeds the company's free cash flow. Access to capital markets is needed for much of large cap public equity markets, and company prospects can sink or swim based on that access to capital markets. Nothing can shut off a company from capital quicker than a broken balance sheet, where excessive leverage causes lenders and investors to panic. Responsible dividend growth companies cannot sustain their dividend intentions if their balance sheet renders such payments vulnerable at the slightest hit to free cash flow. They cannot pay out generously to shareholders if debt service obligations surpass a threshold of safety.

Investing in a post-2008 world should mean aggressively avoiding companies living on the edge financially. The companies who have chosen to function as responsible dividend payers and dividend growers are, by definition, not living on the edge financially. They present a significant reduction of the very existential risk investors ought to be most fearful of.

In companies committed to responsible and sustainable dividend growth, you have a certain insight into the fundamentals of the company, a data point that transcends arbitrary book values, and a signal from management as to what it believes about the sustainability of its dividend growth and, therefore, of its earnings. When the dividend growth pool is limited to those with the free cash flow to responsibly function as such, you significantly decrease the risk of over-leveraged catastrophes and balance sheet horror stories. The type of company that can reasonably be a consistent dividend grower cannot be one that bounces from one cyclical or seasonal product cycle to the next. The highly volatile consumer discretionary space has very few dividend growers for this very reason—constituents are often highly leveraged, and their industry is almost by definition seasonal, cyclical, and faddish. A reliably growing dividend is hard to pay when the company's product is clothing for teenage girls; but when the end product or service that feeds a company's revenue stream is less cyclical, a dependable dividend becomes more feasible. That is not to say that there cannot be "lumpiness" in the cash flows of a dividend growth company, but rather that the dividend is generally set "beneath" the lumpiness, so as to be realistic, attractive, and sustainable.

A final point I would make about the companies we get to buy when we buy companies who prudently pay and grow dividends is that they bring shareholders into alignment with management. It is not my contention that such alignment is not possible without dividend growth, but it is my contention that such alignment is more detectable, stable, and protected when there is a shareholder-friendly policy of dividend growth.

We will quantify the measurably lower volatility that dividend growers have endured versus the broad market in Chapter 6, but my comments here are more philosophical than quantitative. The psychology of the "C suite" for long-term dividend growers has proven to be different from that of much of corporate America. Shareholders are respected by nature of the fact that they are continually rewarded for the risk they take in owning the company. Respect for shareholder risk is one of the most "aligning" things management can do. Belief that shareholders exist to blindly support whatever experimental ideas management may have in their stewardship of company assets is as non-aligning as any belief could be. Dividend payments to shareholders put the shareholders in the front of management's mind each and every quarter. Companies earnestly seeking ways to grow such dividends have a healthy focus on what management has been hired to do: create value through a sustainable and growing enterprise.

In my many years of studying companies on behalf of a professional investment management process, I have become convinced that the culture of companies where dividend growth is valued is different. I believe that the very DNA of a company is different when it seeks to reward shareholders, and then reward them more next year, and more the year after that. Companies with a high short-term focus may think they are rewarding shareholders, but short-term focuses do not build sustainable value for shareholders. A pathology of shareholder value and investor alignment is highly compatible with a dividend growth orientation. Are there good actors in the C-suites of non-dividend growers? Of course! And are there bad actors within dividend growth companies? I am certain there are. But speaking in terms of purposeful generalities and cultural propensities, investors expose themselves to higher quality companies with higher quality management when they pursue companies who have chosen to reward shareholders with growing dividends.

As we will see in the chapters to come, those dividends represent something tangible and powerful for both the accumulator and withdrawer. But nothing means more than the access to quality companies that dividend growth investing represents.

# 4

## ACCUMULATION OF WEALTH

### The Eighth Wonder of the World, on Steroids

*"I don't know what the seven wonders of the world are, but I know the eighth, compound interest."*

—BARON ROTHSCHILD

I am thoroughly convinced that there are two predominant emotions or character traits that govern the investing habits of nearly all investors: *Fear* and *Greed*. The substantial preponderance of investing mistakes come from these two facets of human nature.

The existence of fear when things are bad is certainly not unnatural; an intuitive tendency to panic is part of human nature. This reality doesn't make it any less destructive (and, I will add, it is a reality that properly trained wealth advisors were put on planet earth to counter-act). On the other side of the same coin is the greed that stems from the euphoria of when things are good—when risk and reality are clouded by what seems and feels like free or easy money. It can be character-based (*"I heard my co-worker bragging about his wild returns, and now I have to find those same wild returns."*) or desperation-based (*"I feel like I am behind in my retirement savings, but if I just have this one big hit, I will be back on track."*), but regardless of the motives driving it, when euphoric greed destroys clarity of mind, good things never happen in investing.

Fear can and will become a factor during an investor's accumulation of wealth, but it's monumentally more likely to surface, and for a human investor to succumb to it, when it comes to the *withdrawal* of accumulated wealth. Chapter 5 will take more time to address the *fear* side of the equation: what dividend growth investing means for the defensive investor when they need defense the most, during the withdrawal/spending years of their financial life. I will argue that dividend growth investing not only provides needed psychological defense from the fear of what can go wrong in investing, but it also provides actual defense—real logistical and mechanical superiority against what investors fear the most (namely, outliving their money, usually because of the negative compounding that withdrawing in a sustained declining market can create). This *defensive benefit* of dividend growth investing speaks to a significant demographic of investors by addressing the fear side of the equation.

But when we discuss the *accumulation* of wealth, we are talking about the offensive side of the ball and we are addressing the greed side of the equation. Investors have any number of ways they can earn the capital that will one day be their source for returning capital to them (or to their heirs or charitable bequests). Whether from inheritance, payroll deferral to a retirement program, traditional savings, asset sales, or any other traditional means of obtaining principal capital, the funds diverted to investment objectives are in pursuit of a rational and attractive return on that capital. And, as this chapter will demonstrate, dividend growth investing offers an embedded, exponential *offensive benefit* that very few fully appreciate.

In the previous chapter, we talked about the fundamental argument: the belief that the better companies are the ones paying cash to shareholders. The quality of the underlying investment matters the most, and the quality argument has been made. This chapter argues for superior mechanics—for the actual mathematical model that dividend growth means for a wealth accumulator. Like most wealth accumulation, the underlying dynamic is called *compounding.* It's seemingly simple math that ultimately results in what some, including this author, at the risk of being hyperbolic, would call a miracle. Let's first do a quick refresher of what *normal compounding* is, as it is a powerful enough dynamic in the cause of wealth accumulation. But then we will look at the *special compounding* that takes place within dividend growth investing.

The basics of compounding are not rocket science. If you have $100 that earns 7% in a year, you have $107 at the end of the year. Simple enough. If it earns 7% again in the second year, you do not have $114. You have the second $7 you earned on the initial $100, yes, and you *also* earned 7% on the $7 that you made in the first year. So instead of $114, you have $114.49. That extra year of compounding just made you $0.49 so far, a half-percent on your initial $100. But the "miracle" of compounding requires the gift of time. Let's play this out for twenty years:

First: $100, earning 7% on itself each year, but not compounding the return (so, 7% on $100 for twenty years in a row):

- ▶ $100 principal
- ▶ $7 × 20 years = $140
- ▶ $240 total capital at the end of twenty years

But now: let's look at $100, earning 7% each year, compounding (where each year the 7% is earned on the number that was itself increased by 7% the year prior):

- ▶ $100 principal
- ▶ $7 year one, $7.49 year two, $8.01 year three, and so on
- ▶ $386.97 total capital at the end of twenty years

So, an additional $147 was added in return from compounding the return, above and beyond the return itself. This is a *105% higher return* than that of the simple 7% per year scenario.

Why is it a miracle?

The investor didn't have to do anything to make it happen; it is just math. If the hypothetical return in our scenario is 7%, the investor gets multiples of 7% and all they had to do to achieve more than the 7% their investment was offering was *nothing*. Well, they had to take whatever risk was embedded in the investment that offered a 7% return. But my point is, to get 147% more return than the 140% offered by 7% X 20 years, the investor didn't have to do anything extra for that premium return beyond letting the math happen. This elegant simplicity is the "miracle" of compounding.

Why do more investors not appreciate the miracle of compounding? If I walked up to someone and said, "you are earning 140% over twenty years, but what if I could earn you 287% over twenty years instead, and all you have to do is own the same investment?" who would say no? When you start talking about 147% return premiums, or 287% returns, people pay attention. And this is all based on the real life math of what we are talking about here. So again, why is this not more appreciated?

The answer is there in our first example of the compounded $100 investment. It earned $7 one year, and $7.49 the second year. Even though it is the exact same mathematical force that will create our 147% return premium and 287% twenty-year return, in one given year, it is a 5% difference: $0.49 more on $100. It's nice, but it is decidedly unsexy. Investors are not conditioned to be excited by the tortoise. They like the hare. They see the hare. It may be the tortoise that ends up with a 147% return premium but, ironically, it happens too simply and too painlessly for investors to fully appreciate it.

Isn't *less pain* good? Isn't the simplicity and elegance of compounding the very essence of wise investing? Why resist it?

Greed. Short term-ism. Ego. Bragging rights. Impatience. There are all sorts of reasons one may prefer a "big spike" to the mathematical beauty of compounded investment growth, but they are all bad reasons. The benefits of compounding are inevitable, based on simple math; however, there is a necessary and immutable relationship between these benefits and *time*. The more time one has, the more enhanced the compounding benefit. Compounding is best when time is the longest. The culture is obsessed with timing, with short term-ism. Something that takes "more time" to get "even better" forces the investor to live within the laws of time and nature—one could argue that the mere appreciation of the compounding miracle requires personal character.

Let's now look to the "next layer" of compounding that dividend growth represents. Compounding is splendid enough when an investor owns an underlying asset (let's call it shares of a dividend growth stock, ABC) and that stock's return compounds over the years. In theory, any stock without a dividend can also benefit from compounding, as long as the presumed return is taking effect.

But for accumulators of capital, dividend growth involves the concept of reinvestment: the receipt of dividends that are automatically *reinvested* into more shares of the same asset that is, itself, compounding, and that is, itself, paying out the consistent dividend. *Compounding for a dividend growth investor means compounding the return of the underlying assets, and the return of the additional shares accumulated via dividends, over long periods of time.* The mathematical result from this process can be simply stunning. And from a practical standpoint, it leads to a wonderful growth of principal and a wonderful future income.

But, we are just getting started with what this actually means to a dividend growth investor.

I used a 7% annual return in my earlier example for a nice and simple illustration. And for the sake of argument, we assumed it was 7% per year, meaning each and every year—not less, and not more for any of the years throughout this hypothetical investment. But when it comes to real life risk asset investing, the "average" return and the "actual" return (year by year) are totally different. No risk asset (stocks, mutual funds) returns the exact same return each and every year. The returns on risk assets, even those that are compounding, are not linear. They fluctuate so that, even if they end up averaging, let's say, 7% per year in one year, the return may be +20%, and in another year it may be down 10%. A sequence of such volatile, fluctuating returns may very well end up averaging 7% per year, but the range of outcomes matters to what the final total return will be.

This may be a good time to interject a comment about "volatility." The average rate of return is what investors allegedly care about, but experience and common sense tells us that the ride they go on to get there matters as well. If the return sequence was +50%, -30% +40%, -35%, +40%, an investor may well be happy with their roughly 7% annualized return, but the roller coaster they went on to get there may not have been very pleasant. Alternatively, if an investor receives a +12%, -4%, +10%, -2%, +9% sequence of returns, their return may be quite close to the other scenario, but their path there was likely far more enjoyable. Additionally, in a less volatile sequence, they also are less exposed to the risk of behavioral mistakes from panic or euphoria. Do not misunderstand: volatility is unavoidable for an equity investor, and it should be embraced as a primary source of risk premium. However, all things being equal, a lower volatility ride creating one's return objective is preferable to the same return objective via higher volatility.

What does this have to do with dividend growth investing? It is worth noting that the average variance of returns in dividend growing stocks has been much less than that of the overall market. I will cover this (and the reasons for it) in Chapter 6. However, apart from the argument of a better "volatility-considered" return with dividend growth investing, we do have a real wonder in front of us when we look at what the volatility of returns means for dividend reinvestment compounding.

For an accumulator, a dividend growth investor *benefits* from the volatility of value in the underlying assets because they are mechanically and systematically adding more shares at lower prices during periods of market distress. When market prices recover to normalized return levels, those reinvested shares are worth more money, and they themselves (combined with the initial principal) are all adding greater income and reinvestment of income for the investor. The longer the time period, the greater number of periods of "market distress" one will inevitably face. An investor receiving dividends during those periods, and automatically reinvesting them, is turning market downturns from a "period to patiently wade through" to a "period of enhancing long-term returns" in both principal value and future cash flow.

A hypothetical equity portfolio yielding 4%, with annual appreciation of 5%, and an annual dividend growth of 5% (all hypothetical, but certainly reasonable assumptions for our purposes), would result in 2.76 shares owned for every one share originally purchased21 for a person reinvesting dividends. Again, this is just the math of dividend reinvestment combined with compounding. To understand what functional leverage this has given the investor: they will now achieve a +2.76% return for every 1% gain in the underlying portfolio. The added shares compounding in concert with the compounding of the initial shares results in a miniature compounding machine! Add to the above formula the reality of a 5% annual appreciation that is *not linear* and will involve *periods of negative price fluctuation,* you then add to the mix the fact that more shares will be added in down periods, which will themselves compound and distribute more shares.

You have two dynamics taking place simultaneously at this point:

- ▸ One is the fundamentals of a company servicing their customers, innovating and competing in the market-place and generating the profits that serve as the motive for the entire process. The engines of free enterprise are at work, and create the possibility that an investor can benefit from such a mechanism. As companies compete and earn, investors benefit from the obvious by-product of profit realization.
- ▸ The second is taking place in concert with the first: the mechanical, mathematical beauty of compounded growth and reinvestment of dividends.

It is all for naught if the first element is not there—a successful, competitive business is top priority. But the second element matters, too, for those investors looking to monetize their investment objectives. A successful company owned in public stock markets may achieve dramatic price appreciation over time, but to gain the performance leverage that dividend reinvestment offers, one would need a return multiples higher than the return of the dividend growth portfolio. How does one get a return that is multiples higher? Well, best case, with "multiples higher" risk.

The "Yield on Original Investment" (YOI) concept in Chapter 1 is only possible because of this structural math advantage. Dividends pay over the years. The growing profits and growing dividends of the company cause its own stock price (your original investment) to grow. Throughout the years, the dividends buy more shares (often at lower prices than its median price trajectory would create because of market volatility), and those shares themselves pay a continually growing dividend stream. As these market realities compound and fluctuate throughout time, the result is that cash flow generation compounds and creates a YOI that may be significantly higher than your actual return aspiration itself! Consider the following outcomes, which are charted in Figure 4–1:[22]

► A stock paying a 3% yield and growing the dividend 10% per year, ends up paying a 65% yield each year relative to the original investment amount in its twenty-fifth year of ownership, and over 30% in the twentieth year.

► A stock paying a 4.5% yield and growing the dividend at 6% per year, is quite comparable!

**FIGURE 4–1**

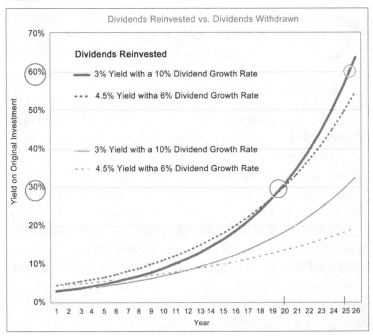

The mathematics of compounding the reinvesting dividends does more than merely create an attractive long-term investment result. There also ought to be an enhanced peace of mind during periods of market volatility, knowing that what is taking place is actually *growing* the investor's future income. How does a declining market help an accumulator and grow their future income? It provides them a larger base of shares (more stock) that will itself be paying needed dividends in the future. For a behaviorally aligned and self-interested, aware investor, this means that market downturns can actually be desired, not feared.

Lowell Miller puts it this way:

> *As we know, mature companies pay dividends from their earnings.... The feature...is that a significant number of companies that raise their dividend every year (or nearly every year). To most, this seems merely a nice amenity, but because most people don't have a long-horizon worldview, they totally underestimate the potency of this factor. It is, in fact, the electricity that will make your compounding machine run. It's the gas for your engine. Dividend growth is the critical piece in the puzzle for creating a portfolio that will serve you over the years.*[23]

What is the downside for the accumulator choosing to gain market returns through the compounding of dividend growth? We already spoke of the obvious reality that *all risk assets* are subject to market volatility. Dividend growth stocks are not immune from price fluctuation when recessions take place, when the monetary base changes, when interest rates move, when geopolitical disruptions take place, and when market sentiment rotates. So, there is the systematic risk of all market prices embedded even in dividend growth stocks, but there is another factor very few accumulators would admit is a concern but which I have seen time and time again in my investing career. And that is the fear of missing a "high flier."

It is not likely that "high fliers" will be found in the space of dividend growing stocks, because as we discussed in the last chapter, the universe of dividend growth stocks is primarily high quality companies in a mature phase of development with defensive characteristics, balance sheet fortitude, and trade largely centered around reliable free cash flow generation. "High fliers" usually fly high because they didn't have balance sheet fortitude to rely on, and didn't have baked in cash flows in their valuation. Rather, they were market disruptors or growth accelerators that achieved an extraordinary market multiple in their valuation. Some see it last and become justified (think of Google and Amazon), for some the jury is still out (think of Netflix), and for some (indeed, most) the high growth valuation eventually comes down to planet earth (in recent years, Twitter and Snap and GoPro are great examples).

I would argue for an accumulator that the avoidance of high fliers is a *blessing*, not a *curse*, because I believe that the pursuit of high fliers leads to more losers than winners through time. Are there investors who *only* bought Facebook and Netflix? I suppose so. But for the most part, the world of high fliers is filled with offsetting success and failure stories, the net result being something more akin to a traditional equity return, with highly amplified volatility.

Yet I am sympathetic to the angst of the equity investor who wants the feeling of "free and quick" money that buying a social media stock at $50 and selling it at $200 can generate. As noted in the beginning of this chapter, greed—or: the euphoric recklessness of ignoring realistic risk/reward trade-offs—is a natural human condition in investing. My suggestion is that the opportunistic, careful, prudent, moderate, fundamental, defensible, repeatable, mathematical, sustainable, and—yes, sometimes "boring"—accumulation of capital via compounding dividend reinvestments is a wonderful governor on the dark side of the human condition when it comes to investing.

Dividend growth equities do not represent 100% of the equity allocations that we manage, though we do tend to pursue a 0% weighting in "high fliers." Where there is room in a portfolio allocation for a non-cash flow generating equity class, we find the emerging markets a more sensible way to pursue "growth" investing. The geopolitical and currency risk embedded in this asset class offers a nice risk premium, and valuations tend to be much lower for much higher internal growth rates. Incidentally, we also find extraordinary secular opportunity for rising dividends out of the emerging markets in the decade to come, as more and more countries and markets find mature governance structures and sophisticated capital structures (see Appendix I).

We also understand that small-cap equity investing can, at times, allow for non-dividend paying (and non-dividend growing) companies, where the focus is on moving from a small company to a large company, and organic management talent and innovation can create opportunity. We do not manage this asset class ourselves, but utilize a specialized manager (same as the aforementioned emerging markets asset class), as we believe the talent to manage this asset class is highly niched, and involves the identification of very particular companies who offer outstanding growth opportunity before the rest of the market has figured it out.

Both emerging markets and small-cap equity are "supplemental" asset classes in the way we construct a portfolio, zero-weighted when a client needs "all hands on deck" in cash flow (income) generation, and often very low-weighted for anyone but those with a high appetite for portfolio value fluctuation. But the core building block of our portfolios for accumulators lies in the dividend growth approach that is proven to offer great growth, great income, and great growth of income. The accumulator may not realize the benefit of the rising income stream now, just like the accumulator does not realize the benefit of the rising prices until they sell, but they build a compounding income stream that simultaneously adds to the value of their principal.

Chapter 6 will make the case that dividend growth investing is hardly a "consolation prize." We believe the return history and return potential for this equity investing approach is, through time, a superior way of investing, even apart from the risk-adjustment (which only adds to its appeal).

But no matter how demonstrable the historical success of dividend growth investing has been, I view the approach as counter-cultural in a day and age that prizes a quick buck the way our culture now does. Easy riches in crypto currency, high flying stock, condo flipping, and dotcom stocks (i.e., 2017, 2013, 2005, 1999, respectively) will always have appeal, and there will never be a shortage of media shows discussing (in hindsight) the "success" stories of such "easy riches." There will never be a shortage of paid salespeople promising more of the same.

To accept a philosophy of dividend growth equity investing is to understand the argument of Chapter 3—that the dividend growth universe consists of a generally superior pool of companies and operators—and then to accept the argument in this chapter—that compounding high quality investments over time, along with the reinvestment of their dividends, is a truly reliable way to accumulate wealth through time. An accumulator who follows this approach, especially with an intellectual understanding of why this works, will have a more peaceful investing life.

It is often said that if investors could only see the earnings and the dividends of the investments they owned, and not the mark-to-market pricing, they would never feel any anxiety at all about their investment portfolio. I would add that if investors who understand the principles of this chapter could see the price fluctuation of their dividend growth stocks, they not only would not feel anxiety but would, in fact, feel great excitement and anticipation.

I am aware of no other investment strategy that has the embedded exploitation of market distress that this does, without having to add new cash! The concept is to allow time, compounding, and the reality of dividend reinvestment to produce a smoother and successful result for your future cash flow needs.

# 5

## WITHDRAWAL MECHANICS MATTER

Avoiding the Poison of Negative Compounding as You Tap Your Nest Egg to Live Happily Ever After

*"If we checked our actual dividend income every 90 days instead of checking our account balances every 90 minutes, we might become better investors."*

—NICK MURRAY

I accept as a fact of life that the significant objective of all investing is the return of cash, in some form or another, at a level greater than the cash that was placed into the investment. As laid out in the Introduction, my first decade in the investment business caused me to seek a way to not just optimally *accumulate capital* on behalf of my clients (as discussed in Chapter 4), but also to find an optimal way to *withdraw capital* for those in the actual realization phase of their ultimate investing objective.

The timing was highly distortive: to enter the investment industry at the peak of the dotcom/tech bubble, followed a few years thereafter by the bursting of a credit and housing bubble that was the largest since the Great Depression. In both cases, the events were technically good for my business as investors had often been under-serviced, poorly-managed, or communicated with ineffectively, and I could change that. The ability to connect with people who were not receiving the advisory experience they needed was pivotal at that stage of my career; in order to fully connect, it was mandatory that I have convictions in sound investment thinking which would properly navigate them through what would become a "lost decade" in capital markets.

Clients deserve confidence and conviction from their wealth managers, but they also deserve for that confidence and conviction to be warranted. High bravado with no substance was not the value proposition investors were looking for in this challenging decade. Substance rooted in fundamental truths and defensible investing principles was the primary need, and once that substance was deeply entrenched in my being, my passion for sharing it was not about to be bridled.

Financial advisors looking to coast are doing their clients a disservice. Careful financial planning, cash flow analysis, and a properly managed portfolio connected to a truly thoughtful plan are the *minimum* of things we ought to be doing. Telling clients what they want to hear is not what they pay me for, and this cuts both ways. I must not tell people that things are all okay if they are not, but I also must not tell people things are terrible if I do not believe they are.

That latter point is actually a far bigger challenge than the former. A significant amount of my politically center-right clients wanted me to tell them from 2009 to 2016 that the market was going to tank because President Obama was in office. I wouldn't do it, for the simple reason that I didn't believe it, and my business is built on trust. I cannot create trust if I fail to be trustworthy, and capitulating in the advice category to say what you know they want to hear is fraudulent—a form of malpractice.

I happened to believe throughout the years of the Obama administration that periods of reflation were generally very positive for markets, and that regardless of where I felt he could have improved regulatory and tax conditions for American markets, the market bottoming of 2008–09 was such that significant price appreciation was likely on the table as corporate profits had bottomed, as had equity valuations. Certain years provided incredible dividend and price growth in the energy pipeline space (2011), other years saw certain companies' dividend yields normalize as prices reverted to normal valuations (2010, 2013), and other years traded in fear of what the Federal Reserve had on its agenda (2014, 2015). I am not arguing that President Obama helped equity markets or hurt them. I am making the point that had I told those who I knew wanted to hear me say it that the mere existence of President Obama in the White House was going to crush equities, I would have done irreparable harm to their financial position and violated my sacred fiduciary duties.

And of course, the same is true (with different political twists) since President Trump took office. The job of a financial advisor is to tell the truth and, frankly, most of the time markets are not impacted by politics. Policy matters, of course, but often policies take effect under strange circumstances (e.g., market friendly policies passed in the Clinton-era 1990s; market destructive policies passed in the Nixon-era 1970s). Partisan correlations are hard to find.

What does politics have to do with withdrawal mechanics of dividend growth investing? Simply this: for me in my career, there has been no greater opportunity to tell people what they want to hear than "Markets will do [fill in the blank] because President [fill in the blank] is in office." And yet I have resisted that pedestrian, dishonest, and cheap approach to client counsel at every turn. If I can resist the allure of reducing my investment advice to people's most crass partisan leanings, then surely I can resist the temptation to *tell people that their withdrawal plans are air tight, even if they are not.*

And I would suggest that a significant portion of the investing public has a withdrawal plan that will prove inadequately constructed through time.

The mistakes around monetization of one's portfolio take various forms. The most obvious would be having the math wrong: assuming one can afford a withdrawal level that is wholly unsustainable, particularly once the impact of taxes and inflation are considered. Return expectations are often assumed that are not indicative of the actual portfolio a given investor has, or are not adequately stress-tested to account for bad timing or other eventualities. But I would argue that the most common mistake is this:

*To plan on a systematic withdrawal from one's portfolio— without adequate cash reserves—presuming the portfolio will offer a linear return rather than a volatile one.*

This mistake is systemic in today's financial planning. Do-it-yourself investors and financial advisors who are not living up to their professional obligations are doing something like this: taking a denominator of assets, assuming a 7-9% constant return rate, and plugging in a withdrawal rate that pencils as being sustainable throughout one's life. "If I earn 8% per year, but withdraw 6% per year, I obviously can make it the rest of my life, and even come out okay."

If only it were that simple. This brings us back to March 2000. There is no easy way to calculate how many people may have retired in the general time frame of 1999–2001, plugged into an equity-heavy portfolio, and commenced a systematic withdrawal plan from their investments. If they did not maintain a "cash bucket" to tap during periods of market distress, the fact of the matter is that they entered a sustained period of what is called "negative compounding." From 2000 to 2008 the market had a negative rate of return (compounding at -1.59% over that nine-year period, including the dividends the S&P 500 offered). Let's look at the principle of this hypothetical scenario using real-life returns and sequences.

I will first offer the following caveats: This is assuming someone is invested 100% in the S&P 500 (I would hope to heavens they would have better diversification than that). Most notably, it assumes they do not alter their withdrawal plans throughout the bloodbath, which is likely unrealistic, but since I am trying to illustrate what can happen to withdrawal strategies without proper planning, it is a worthwhile thought experiment, no matter how violent the outcome). It also does not reflect a "side pocket" of cash that one could tap for a year or two, a defensive planning alternative that would surely make a difference!

In this scenario, someone retires with $2 million, and begins taking $120,000 per year (6% of the initial $2 million) from the portfolio, as pictured in the Figure 5–1.[24] As you can see, after three years, they are down over 50% on the principal balance. The principal holds in place for a few years after that and even recovers $100,000 or so, before coming all the way down to $525,000 by the end of 2008. A portfolio whose investments were

**FIGURE 5–1**

| | | | 6% of beginning value per year | |
|---|---|---|---|---|
| YEAR | Beginning Value | Return | Withdrawal | Ending Balance |
| 2000 | $ 2,000,000 | -9.10% | $ (120,000) | $ 1,698,000.00 |
| 2001 | $ 1,698,000 | -11.89% | $ (120,000) | $ 1,376,108 |
| 2002 | $ 1,376,108 | -22.10% | $ (120,000) | $ 951,988 |
| 2003 | $ 951,988 | 28.68% | $ (120,000) | $ 1,105,018 |
| 2004 | $ 1,105,018 | 10.88% | $ (120,000) | $ 1,105,244 |
| 2005 | $ 1,105,244 | 4.91% | $ (120,000) | $ 1,039,512 |
| 2006 | $ 1,039,512 | 15.79% | $ (120,000) | $ 1,083,650 |
| 2007 | $ 1,083,650 | 5.49% | $ (120,000) | $ 1,023,143 |
| 2008 | $ 1,023,143 | -37.00% | $ (120,000) | $ 524,580 |
| | | -1.59% | Average return, nine years | |

**FIGURE 5–2**

| YEAR | Beginning Value | Return | Withdrawal | Ending Balance |
|------|-----------------|--------|------------|----------------|
| | | | 6% of adjusted value each year | |
| 2000 | $ **2,000,000** | -9.10% | $ (120,000) | $ 1,698,000.00 |
| 2001 | $ 1,698,000 | -11.89% | $ (101,880) | $ 1,394,228 |
| 2002 | $ 1,394,228 | -22.10% | $ (83,654) | $ 1,002,450 |
| 2003 | $ 1,002,450 | 28.68% | $ (60,147) | $ 1,229,805 |
| 2004 | $ 1,229,805 | 10.88% | $ (73,788) | $ 1,289,820 |
| 2005 | $ 1,289,820 | 4.91% | $ (77,389) | $ 1,275,761 |
| 2006 | $ 1,275,761 | 15.79% | $ (76,546) | $ 1,400,658 |
| 2007 | $ 1,400,658 | 5.49% | $ (84,039) | $ 1,393,515 |
| 2008 | $ 1,393,515 | -37.00% | $ (83,611) | $ **794,303** |
| | | **-1.59%** | Average return, nine years | |

down 1.59% per year is actually itself down 75% over nine years—the most insidious form of negative compounding imaginable!

Now let's actually look at it from another perspective, where the retiree does not take their number fixed every year (as a percentage of starting deposit), but lets it fluctuate each year with the value of the portfolio (6% each year). (See Figure 5–2.) Here you see that they end with $794,000, not $525,000, *but* their annual lifestyle has taken as much as a 50% adjustment (2003) and is routinely around 60–70% of desired cash flow. How many of you are interested in a 30–40% downward adjustment to your annual income, while still seeing your principal decline 60% over nine years?

To repeat my caveats, it may very well seem that several knobs could have been turned to avoid these ghastly outcomes. And I concur! As I stated, the use of a cash reserve is but one very effective tool, not to mention the idea of asset allocation within the portfolio so as to not require the entire source of return to be exposed to market risk at all times.

But one could also argue that these simple models do not even capture the full horror of things, for they do not account for two of the three most certain things in life: taxes and inflation!

Factor in a reasonable tax rate on retirement account withdrawals, or investment taxes, and inflate upwards the withdrawal rate to some type of inflation index, and these numbers quickly get much uglier!

If I were to critique my own reasoning here, it would be to point out my rank cherry-picking. I am starting the model at an all-time market valuation high (a bubble, no less), and ending it at the end of the worst crash since the Great Depression. Actually, I end it December 31, 2008; if I let the months of January and February 2009 bleed through, it would have just been too painful to look at it, not to mention too painful to recollect those awful months. But yes, this is cherry-picking, and one is free to dismiss some of the data because of that, if they wish. The problem with doing that, though, is that even if the 2008 drop was hyper-rare, 20–40% drops are not unheard of (2008, 2001–02, 1973–74), and it surely seems appropriate to set the table for *real-life* conditions if our goal is to contrast it to an alternative means of portfolio withdrawal.

I am not making the argument that "2008 will happen again, so therefore a different withdrawal plan is needed." In fact, I am making no argument about market returns whatsoever. Rather, I am simply suggesting a different *framework*, not market outlook. If I were only discussing market outlooks, I would be discussing the pivotal need to be exposed to market returns. For bear markets notwithstanding, equity risk premium is the building block of any investment portfolio, an irreplaceable inflation hedge that has created incalculable amounts of wealth.

My point is not to flee the volatility (and therefore the returns) of equities. Quite the contrary. Rather, it is to embrace the upside of equities while simultaneously, in the withdrawal phase of one's financial life, considering a different mechanism that will not expose one to the reality of negative compounding.

The years 2000–2008 happened to reflect two dramatic bookends of market declines. The period 1966–1981, on the other hand, did not necessarily experience the same market decline components, but did experience prolonged periods of flat market returns, if divorced from the income of the portfolio! In other words, reliance on linear price appreciation has plenty of precedents for being an inadequately thoughtful withdrawal strategy.

In the previous chapter, we explored the (math) miracle of compounding, and the double miracle that compounding reinvested dividends represents. One entering the withdrawal phase of their financial life very likely has to forego the growth benefit of dividend reinvestment. Instead, it is time to get paid! Rather than using dividends as a means to acquire more future dividends, it is time to use dividends to pay for food, presents for the grandkids, and cruises in the Caribbean.

The first antidote to the negative compounding of withdrawing linear dollars from a non-linear return portfolio is this: dividends are never, ever negative. One's total portfolio return may be +10% and it may be -10%, but a dividend yield can only be 0% or higher. The greater the portion of one's withdrawal coming from the dividend (my preferred portion is 100% of the withdrawal, if the asset denominator and dividend yield are sufficient to allow such), the less negative compounding that can mathematically take place.

What happened to the dividend yield of the S&P 500 during the 2000–2002 market crash? The dividends paid out from the index were practically flat, but to the extent that they were lower than the previous year, it was a low single-digit decline (roughly 3%). But keep in mind that was still a positive number—the cash being paid out was a positive addition to the portfolio, where the price level was a declining number (nearly 50% over those three years, to be precise).

Using the dividend yield of the S&P 500 to make my point assures that my argument can only get better from there. The whole point of writing a book about dividend growth investing is to advocate for dividend growth investing—not holding over a hundred companies that pay no dividend at all, and another 250 companies that pay insignificant or non-growing dividends. If my point has legs with *just S&P dividends and yield characteristics*, how much more so with an intentional portfolio focused on true dividend growth!

Indeed, we seek to remedy the inconvenient schedule of market returns, not market returns themselves. Dividends help us remedy two areas of concern: the nature of returns (price appreciation can be negative; dividends cannot) and the schedule of returns (price appreciation is sporadic even when positive; dividends are linear and dependable).

I will discuss in Chapter 9 the ways in which dividend cuts can and must be avoided. I make no claims that this approach can be passively replicated with great ease. But for our purposes in this chapter (to merely evaluate an alternative mechanical means of withdrawing from an investment portfolio to realize income/cash flow needs), presuppose a portfolio objective that is successful in avoiding dividend reductions in aggregate. In this scenario, the retiree will have achieved two tremendous things (and actually more):

1. They can insulate themselves against the concerns of market fluctuations. The price level may be zigging and zagging, but the income is growing, nice and steady, regardless.
2. They can also achieve an actual pay increase, year-over-year. A dividend growth portfolio is to return, well, dividend growth (i.e. growth of the dividends themselves). Retirees do not want the income reduced, nor do

they want to deplete their principal when withdrawals exceed market returns in tough market conditions. But they have another objective as well: to have income grow! Chapter 7 will thoroughly unpack the idea of dividend growth as the ultimate inflation defense, but for now my point is merely mathematical. Cash flow is growing from the portfolio regardless of market conditions, and this enables the investor to enjoy what that represents, with an agnostic view of market prices.

It occurs to me that I am being quite unfair to pick on non-dividend stocks or broad market indices as the only inferior alternative to dividend growth investing when it comes to withdrawing from a portfolio of assets. For indeed, one of the even more common strategies than systematic withdrawals from the S&P 500 is the belief that bonds can accomplish the income need (i.e. fixed income).

The tremendous flaw with "fixed" income is, of course, the fact that it is "fixed." Inflation and taxes mean the withdrawal need is not fixed, it is growing. But bonds force you to withdraw from principal, and to do so without even the hope of offsetting growth. Our prior dissection of the S&P 500 outcome may have reflected a declining principal because of market conditions, but at least there was *hope* and *opportunity* for offsetting growth! With bonds, one will deteriorate principal to have the income keep up with escalating withdrawal needs, and they will do so with no possibility of portfolio appreciation to offset.

Additionally, the contemporary environment matters, too. Bonds no longer offer an income level that can be considered an adequate substitute. With the ten-year treasury yield anchored below 3%, investors face both inadequate coupon and interest rate risk to prices if and when rates rise. It is a highly asymmetrical risk vs. reward trade-off.

Note: this is not to say that bonds have no role in a portfolio; we are asset allocators and advocate for appropriate diversification in line with each investor's unique liquidity needs and tolerance for volatility. What I am criticizing, though, is the idea of using *fixed* income to create a *fluctuating* withdrawal. The math doesn't work!

So what are we envisioning? Substantively, how would a withdrawal strategy work for a dividend growth portfolio, versus the systematic withdrawal approach so many are either consciously or unintentionally practicing?

As Figure 5–3 indicates, the concept is to create a consistent linear deposit into the investor's checking account, in line with their monthly cash flow need. Hypothetically, they could have $15,000 of monthly spending need, with $5,000 of outside income (social security, pensions, royalties, etc.) so a net need

**FIGURE 5–3**

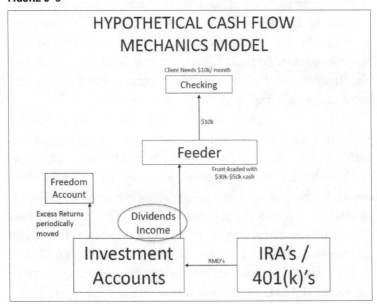

## HYPOTHETICAL CASH FLOW MECHANICS MODEL

Client Needs $10k/ month

Checking

$10k

Feeder

Front-loaded with
$30k-$50k cash

Freedom
Account

Excess Returns
periodically
moved

Dividends
Income

Investment
Accounts

RMD's

IRA's /
401(k)'s

from the portfolio of $10,000 per month (again, this is a hypothetical, as portfolio values and spending needs fluctuate depending on individual needs, lifestyles, resources, etc.). What you see below is a "feeder" account consisting of a cash reserve that receives all dividends from the investment account, and "feeds" the fixed amount to the client's outside checking account monthly. The value of the investment account can and will fluctuate (though, as has been discussed, it is not expected to do so to the same degree higher beta portfolios would), but it is an immaterial input to the client's receipt of cash flow. The "shares" are left intact in the investment portfolio (as sales are not needed to support the withdrawal), and the income created flows into the feeder to create a linear and dependable withdrawal. Now, some people want additional spending resources beyond their monthly needs (i.e. special vacations, boats, cars, toys, grandkids) and this plan, because it involves risk assets, not fixed income "par" instruments, should be creating excess returns (above and beyond the dividends) through time. The ability to tactically and intelligently realize gains from time to time in consultation with the client and their need affords the advisor the ability to feed the "freedom" account as well, but never at a time when market returns are negative.

The basic program requires modification. Real granular financial planning is needed to solve for that withdrawal need. It also should allow for periodic increases to offset inflation. "Cash reserve" in the "feeder" account will vary, based on liquidity needs, the size of the investment portfolio relative to the withdrawal need, and a client's own "sleep at night" comfort level. Charitable planning may be relevant around the required IRA distributions. In fact, for some investors the asset denominator is heavily weighted towards pre-tax accounts, and may require a tax sensitivity in the impact of withdrawals. Again, these details can be addressed on a case-by-case basis as part of a really comprehensive financial plan.

The point is to simply create a mechanism whereby one is protected from the reality of negative compounding. You show me an investment plan that seeks to consistently spend "portfolio gains" and I will show you a vulnerable investment plan exposed to negative compounding. Spending from an appreciating portfolio in a bull market (say, 1982–1999, or 2009–2018) may work out just fine, though even then, it may not be the most tax-efficient (but I digress). However, many in the withdrawal stage of their financial lives do not want to fret over whether we are in a secular bull market or not. And in fact, all bull markets feature plenty of zigs, zags, jolts of reality, and other such hiccups.

In fact, consider the *average* intra-year downside market volatility, even in the midst of really good markets! Intra-year declines of 7–18% are not merely possible, even in years where the market has a very good return; they are probable! You have years like 1995 and 2017 where the worst peak-to-trough decline of the market is 3%, but median level downside volatility is over 10%. (See Figure 5–4.) That means the sequence of withdrawals matters, and positive dividend growth gives us the ability to manage this process, better protect client capital, and still seek growing income regardless of market environment!

This mechanical benefit does not exist in isolation. Positive cash flow growth to withdraw from in volatile markets is a significant benefit, but it also stands next to the overall portfolio quality argument, the reduced volatility reality, and the hedge against rising expenses. It is all of these benefits in concert with one another that make the collective case for dividend growth equities.

Our purpose in this chapter was to illustrate the benefits of turning the dial off of "dividend reinvestment" and on to "dividend withdrawal," so as to replace the status quo approach of

**FIGURE 5–4**

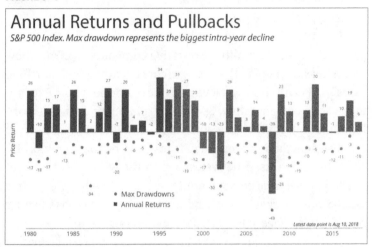

## Annual Returns and Pullbacks
*S&P 500 Index. Max drawdown represents the biggest intra-year decline*

"financing a constant, nonvolatile spending plan using a risky, volatile investment strategy."[25]

It strikes this author as indescribably bizarre that the two most common methods of monetizing withdrawals are:

1. Linear withdrawals from equity prices, which are very subject to decline, and
2. Linear withdrawals from bond coupons, which are very subject to decline.

When a third option exists

3. Linear or fluctuating withdrawals (your choice) from equity dividends, not subject to decline.

The superiority in option three should be self-evident: freedom of choice in the amount withdrawn—a constant amount or a fluctuating one (meaning, fluctuating *up*). And, the elimination of the great risk that options one and two inherently possess: exposure to decline in the element being withdrawn upon for cash flow needs.

I am well aware that dividends are not guaranteed, but we are not talking about outlier events when we talk about S&P price volatility or bond yield declines. A ten-year treasury currently pays one-third as much as it did when I was born in 1974. The S&P 500's volatility has been well-established (and as an accumulator, is something I very much embrace). But where, I ask you, is the precedent for dividend growers cutting their dividends? More importantly, before one pulls an isolated case from 2008 here or there, where is the precedent for a diversified portfolio of dividend growing stocks seeing its cash distribution cut? You will try in vain to answer.

No discussion of this topic will ever come to a different conclusion than this: the less you withdraw from principal, the longer your money will last. Our goal as dividend growth investors is to feed the cash flow needs of our clients today, as well as tomorrow. With "tomorrow" now covering longer and longer periods of time, the stakes are higher to ensure that one's investment strategy during any withdrawal period has durability and common sense. A withdrawal of a robust, growing stream of dividends offers both.

# 6

## OPPORTUNITY COST MYTH

### Why Dividend Growth Investing Is Not a Return Consolation Prize

*"We believe that, in general, compounding income over time—not style, sector, or asset class—is the most reliable driver of long-term returns."*

—MILLER/HOWARD INVESTMENTS

The last three chapters have all focused on various arguments in favor of dividend growth investing: the superior quality of companies that are often represented, the mathematical benefit of compounding returns with reinvested dividends, and finally, the protective benefits of withdrawing from a positive cash flow instead of a potentially negative price component. All of these arguments are powerful in their own right, but when taken as a whole explain the force of my conviction for dividend growth equities.

This chapter can be taken as an additional argument in favor of the strategy if you wish—that the long-term performance has been stellar—but that is actually not my intent. I do not argue for any investment strategy based on its past track record, as that argument would necessarily be implying that the past says something to us about the future. The fact of the matter is that there are plenty of reasons to form opinions about what the future will look like, but the mere fact of what happened in the past is not one of them. Perhaps past performance helps to validate a narrative, or create a probability structure, but it is not an isolated argument about the future. This is not a mere mantra for the compliance departments of the world; it is a fact. There are reasons to believe that innovative companies with strong business models and competitive advantages, who diligently manage their capital structure and balance sheet, and who are growing free cash flows will be able to continue paying generous dividends to shareholders and see their share prices rise through time. Those reasons are fundamental; they are logical; they are economic; and they are evidence-based. But that is categorically different from stating, "the past did this so, therefore, the future will too."

The reason to delve into the performance history of dividend growth stocks is not to formulate a separate argument for the space but, rather, to empirically respond to an argument that may be made against it. That argument goes something like this:

*"Sure, you create a smoother withdrawal strategy when you pull from dividends, and, yes, there are plenty of safer companies in the dividend growth category, but the cost of these added benefits is that you will give up some meaningful amount of return."*

The argument warrants a response, for indeed, some investors—thus far interested in the arguments I have made for this approach to equity investing—may be turned off if it meant that the price they would pay for the benefits of this approach is a meaningful reduction in total return. We are going to resort to evidence to at least look at what the past has said about all of this—not to tell people what to think about the future, but, rather, to tell them what to think about, well, the past!

And, in addition, to understand the actual "offense" of dividend growth investing, I will seek to unpack it all in a context of risk and volatility. The big picture matters.

Nine years into an equity bull market, it makes sense that some investors may wonder if they need *any* approach to stock market investing other than just "buying the market." Indeed, for some investors in recent years, they may not even believe they need the whole market. If past performance were indicative of future results, an all-FANG[26] portfolio would be perfectly adequate!

There are two possible responses one may have to the post-crisis conditions of the stock market, and I believe both are problematic.

One is to assert that any pursuit of isolated investment criteria (such as dividend growing companies) is unnecessary and unhelpful because buying the whole market will do the job just fine. Furthermore, in years like 2013 (when the S&P 500 was up 30%) and 2017 (when the S&P 500 was up 20%), very few particular strategies are going to beat the index's performance anyways. (See Figure 6–1.) Therefore, the whole pursuit of a nuanced approach is futile.

This response is fine on the surface. I do not dispute the long-term track record of the S&P 500, and I certainly do not dispute the performance since 2009. Now, an investor who will look at the whole picture may be a little surprised at the data. For example, the total return since 2009 of the S&P 500 market index is a stunning 15% (annually). But pull up to a higher level and you see a nearly two-decade return of just about 7% per year (including dividends, of course). (See Figure 6–2.)

Oh, and to reiterate the importance of dividends, even in a non-dividend focused portfolio:

*The price-only return of the S&P 500 since 2000: 5% per year*

**FIGURE 6–1**

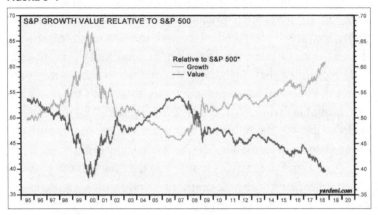

| Macrotrends Data | |
|---|---|
| S&P 500 Historical Annual Returns | |
| www.macrotrends.net | |
| 2017 | 21.83% |
| 2016 | 11.96% |
| 2015 | 1.38% |
| 2014 | 13.69% |
| 2013 | 32.39% |
| 2012 | 16.00% |
| 2011 | 2.11% |
| 2010 | 15.06% |
| 2009 | 26.46% |
| 2008 | -37.00% |
| 2007 | 5.49% |
| 2006 | 15.79% |
| 2005 | 4.91% |
| 2004 | 10.88% |
| 2003 | 28.68% |
| 2002 | -22.10% |
| 2001 | -11.89% |
| 2000 | -9.10% |
| **15.65% 2009-2017** | |
| **7.03% 2000-2017** | |

**FIGURE 6–2**

This is one of the huge reasons why disingenuous life insurance or annuity products that offer the return of the index, with dividends stripped out, should be avoided like the plague. Imagine giving up 29% of the return over a twenty-year period!

The argument that an index-only return is adequate for the needs of all investors is fine, as long as the mechanics of compounding are understood, the mechanics of withdrawals (as discussed in the last chapter) are understood, and the realities of index volatility are understood. My argument in this book is not about the inadequacy of index returns; it is about the optimization available through dividend growth equities. And this chapter seeks to answer the objection that optimization comes with the cost of lower performance. The facts will show otherwise.

The second potential response one may have to the post-crisis conditions of the stock market is even more dangerous—to allow for a nuanced parsing of the index towards a more particular investment outcome, but to do it *not* by seeking to simplify and optimize around a philosophy like dividend growth, but rather to find those "hot dots" whose momentum surely mean they can do no wrong. "Cult stocks" often create incorrigibly stubborn investors, and like the dotcom era of the late 1990s, the FANG era of 2013–18 has led some investors to believe that investment principles have been re-written altogether.

Indeed, one high-tech growth manager had this to say about utilizing "value" investing in this "new economy":

> *"Value investing is a lost cause in today's high-tech, winner-take-all economy. The world we live in today—it is haves and have-nots, and there are way more have-nots. There are so many industries being disrupted by the digitization of the world; it's hard to make cyclical bets on have-not value stocks."*[27]

Buying the highest performer in a given period after it has been the highest performer in a given period has not, historically, ended well in that next given period. Put differently, "rearview mirror" investing—buying yesterday's winners, today, because they were yesterday's winners—will always work, until it doesn't. Just as picking an exact bottom is not easy to do, often a rearview mirror/momentum investor may buy before a top is found, giving credence to their newfound genius as a stock picker (when the high momentum stocks continue their upward climb). But when things set in, "genius" gets revealed for what it was.

My beef is not with growth stocks (who wouldn't want to own companies that are growing their profits?) and it is not with any particular companies such as those referred to as FANG. Rather, it is with a conscious investment policy of hot-dot selection, which is highly exposed to selection risk, timing risk, and the fundamental contrarian reality that when everyone else starts to do something, the life cycle of that investment approach may be in very late innings.

One's view of performance is always and forever a by-product of the timeline in which one is looking. There is no reason for advocates of my investing worldview to deny that in certain periods, dividend growing stocks are highly likely to underperform other aspects of the market. The years 1999 and 2013 are extreme examples of high growth outshining everything else, but there are other periods as well. But as we will see, when one steps outside short-term windows and looks to more appropriate long-term windows, the facts become abundantly clear.

Isn't appealing to the "long term" the convenient escape for all underperformance? In the long run aren't we all dead, as John Maynard Keynes famously reminded us? There may be a convenient tendency to default to long term references in certain contexts, but it bears repeating that the entire argument I have centered this thesis around is the notion of "Yield on Original Investment," the future income generation one can receive from a high-quality dividend grower when compounding reinvested dividends is allowed to take place. This is, by definition, a long-term paradigm. I want to demonstrate the long-term track record of dividend-growing stocks because I believe in long-term accumulation periods (twenty-, thirty-, and forty-year periods), and

I believe in long term withdrawal periods (twenty-, thirty-, and forty-year periods). Someone who accumulates money until age sixty has very likely been saving in a 401k account for thirty to thirty-five years, and will be withdrawing money from age sixty to ninety, or ninety-five, or more.

In other words, if you are fifty-seven years old and looking for the hottest sector to invest in for twelve months, or twenty-four months, or thirty-six months, I confess that I have no opinion as to whether or not dividend growers will outperform other types of stocks in such time periods. But I will remind you: no one else has any idea what will perform best for that one-, two-, or three-year period either! I am not suggesting that the three-year projected return is irrelevant to that fifty-seven-year-old investor (though it probably is), but I am suggesting that it is irrelevant to any fiduciary advisor trying to do what is best for her clients. Such short-term windows are highly susceptible to reality, and reality involves geopolitics, monetary policy, unexpected market disruptions, news scandals, global conditions, and psychology and sentiment. What I am describing is "noise." Why would anyone want to make projections around "noise"? I am not merely referring to the risk of getting "noise" wrong; I am referring to the *inevitability* of getting noise wrong! If noise could be forecasted, predicted, traded, avoided, or exploited, it wouldn't be noise!

Looking at longer-term realities in dividend growth investing is not avoidance behavior—it is prudent and wise. And I cannot make clear enough: longer term windows are *especially* significant when it comes to the very ethos of dividend growth investing, when the underlying tenets are management's stewardship of the finances, the maturity and stability of the business model, the ability to withstand various unforeseen troubles that arise, and the positive return component that provides offset to the price volatility. All of these things, philosophically and mathematically, are suited for long-term analysis.

Another important illustration: let's compare a strong dividend sector to the hottest stock market sector in history—a largely non-dividend paying one, the great, vaulted technology sector! Investors are no doubt aware of the world-changing advancements in technology over the last few decades. Indeed, more progress has taken place in technology in the last twenty years than had taken place in the ten thousand years that preceded them! In fact, the Nasdaq and its heavy technology composition have been so incredibly positioned for growth and innovation that it has outperformed—on a price basis—the boring utilities sector by 6,400% since 1971, when the Nasdaq and the technology boom began. (See Figure 6–3.)

But wait. What about when dividends get added into the mix? We all know that utilities are boring, have little price growth, and are, well, utilities. Technology is the lifeblood of the economy, has created a digital revolution, and represents the biggest growth sector in the market, right? Well, let's take a look at utilities vs. technology since I was born—in this, the strongest technology era in history.[28] (See Figure 6–4.)

The total return of the boring utility sector is 800% higher in my lifetime than the exciting, growth-oriented Nasdaq! This amounts to a +0.21% increase in return, annually. And of course, this superior return result has taken place with a tiny, tiny fraction of the price volatility!

**FIGURE 6–3**

| | CCMP | ↓ 7227.289 | +139.138 | | |
|---|---|---|---|---|---|
| | At 14:47 | O 7065 671 | H 7228.263 | L 7057 | |
| CCMP Index | | | 97) Settings | | |
| Range | 02/25/1971 | | 03/30/2018 | | |
| Security | | Currency | | Price Change | |
| 1) CCMP Index | | USD | | 6870.05% | |
| 2) UTIL Index | | USD | | 470.44% | |

**FIGURE 6–4**

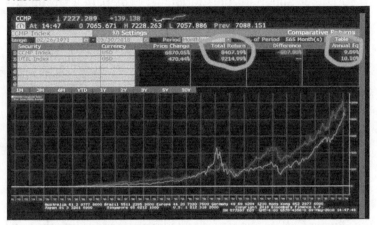

Am I suggesting that utilities are a better total return investment than technology? Of course not. I am demonstrating that even in an unfair match (the high growth of tech vs. the low growth of utilities), given enough time, the positive contribution of *income* becomes a mathematically irresistible force in total return. I have no doubt that in certain periods the outperformance of technology over utilities would be monumental. But this is a very long-term demonstration in a period where technology has completely flourished. And yet....

It is nothing more than the math of reinvested income. Utilities may only be up 470% in over forty years, but the constant flow of positive cash into the mix created a compounded result that is surely as shocking to you as it was to me.

Ned Davis Research has done industry-leading research to further unpack the long-term track record of dividend growth. The results continually demonstrate a similar theme: improved performance, with reduced volatility.

Figure 6–5 demonstrates the returns and volatility of stocks segmented by dividend policy. Figure 6–6 is updated through

## FIGURE 6–5

## FIGURE 6–6

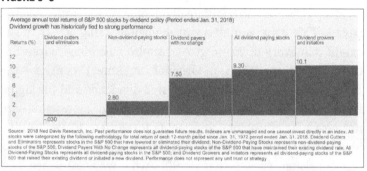

early 2018 numbers, and even adds the agony of dividend cutters to the mix.

Initially, this groundbreaking research was shocking. Market analysts expected that the dividend sector represented a lower volatility mode of investing, but higher returns to boot? The surprise stemmed from an inadequate appreciation of the role of reinvested income in the long-term result of an investment.

Allow me to reiterate why the volatility is reduced in dividend-focused sectors. Yes, I do believe there is an inherently more stable return result when there is positive income offsetting some of the price fluctuation, and when the companies tend to have more stable income statements and balance sheets. But mathematics is at play as well. Volatility is naturally reduced when 50–75% of the return objective cannot go below 0%! If we are trying to get an 8% return, and half of it will be from a 4% dividend, and half will come from price, we only have downside volatility in 50% of our return. But if one is trying to get an 8% return with no dividend yield (for example, FANG) or with a 1.5–2% yield (for example, the S&P 500), then there will be price fluctuation around 75–100% of the return. The return could very well end up being as good (and in certain periods, better), but it can *only* do so with heightened price fluctuation. (See Figure 6–7.)

I also want to differentiate dividend growers from dividend payers. This book is only about dividend paying stocks to the extent that every dividend grower is also a dividend payer. But truth be told, the "Yield on Original Investment" concept—the full power of compounding reinvested dividends and the signal from management that a growing dividend represents—are not nearly as efficacious arguments for a mere "payer" of dividends; they find full force when the dividend is growing! It is that consistent growth that signifies what we want to see, and creates the logistical effect we want created for accumulators and withdrawers.

**FIGURE 6–7**

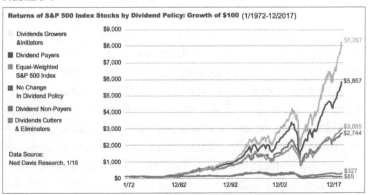

Returns of S&P 500 Index Stocks by Dividend Policy: Growth of $100 (1/1972-12/2017)

## FIGURE 6–8

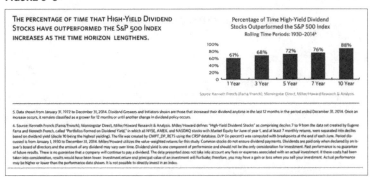

THE PERCENTAGE OF TIME THAT HIGH-YIELD DIVIDEND
STOCKS HAVE OUTPERFORMED THE S&P 500 INDEX
INCREASES AS THE TIME HORIZON LENGTHENS.

Percentage of Time High-Yield Dividend
Stocks Outperformed the S&P 500 Index
Rolling Time Periods: 1930–2014[6]

Source: Kenneth French (Fama/French), Morningstar Direct, Miller/Howard Research & Analysis.

5. Data shown from January 31, 1972 to December 31, 2014. Dividend Growers and Initiators shown are those that increased their dividend anytime in the last 12 months in the period ended December 31, 2014. Once an increase occurs, it remains classified as a grower for 12 months or until another change in dividend policy occurs.

6. Source: Kenneth French (Fama/French), Morningstar Direct, Miller/Howard Research & Analysis. Miller/Howard defines "High-Yield Dividend Stocks" as comprising deciles 7 to 9 from the data set created by Eugene Fama and Kenneth French, called "Portfolios Formed on Dividend Yield," in which all NYSE, AMEX, and NASDAQ stocks with Market Equity for June of year t, and at least 7 monthly returns, were separated into deciles based on dividend yield (decile 10 being the highest yielding). The file was created by CMPT_DP_RETS using the CRSP database. D/P (in percent) was computed with breakpoints at the end of each June. Period discussed is from January 1, 1930 to December 31, 2014. Miller/Howard utilizes the value-weighted returns for this study. Common stocks do not ensure dividend payments. Dividends are paid only when declared by an issuer's board of directors and the amount of any dividend may vary over time. Dividend yield is one component of performance and should not be the only consideration for investment. Past performance is no guarantee of future results. There is no guarantee that a company will continue to pay a dividend. The data presented does not take into account any fees or expenses associated with an actual investment. If these costs had been taken into consideration, results would have been lower. Investment return and principal value of an investment will fluctuate; therefore, you may have a gain or loss when you sell your investment. Actual performance may be higher or lower than the performance data shown. It is not possible to directly invest in an index.

The long-term results from a performance standpoint are most potent in this space as well.

The amount of time a dividend focus like this may underperform the S&P 500 depends entirely on the time period being evaluated. Figure 6–8 indicates that the longer the time period, the more likely it is that dividend stocks will outperform the S&P 500 (61% of the time in a one-year time horizon; 88% of the time in a ten-year time horizon).

The argument of this chapter is rebuttal-driven rather than affirmative. I am not arguing that dividend growth stocks are going to outperform in the years ahead. I am, however, arguing against the notion that they will underperform by pointing to history. (See Figure 6–9.) The future is unknowable, and it is for that reason that we prefer to stack the deck with as much security and stability as we can. If we do not know what the markets will do, in general, we really do not know what unproven, untested, unseasoned financial operators will do.

The dividend growth universe gives us two embedded benefits we find attractive:

1. Management that is aligned with shareholders and managing the income statement to create stable, growing earnings; and,

**FIGURE 6-9**

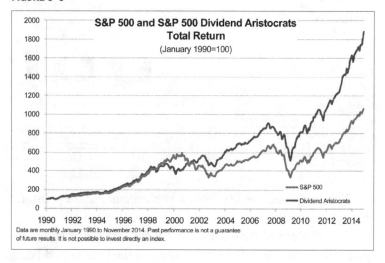

S&P 500 and S&P 500 Dividend Aristocrats
Total Return
(January 1990=100)

Data are monthly January 1990 to November 2014. Past performance is not a guarantee
of future results. It is not possible to invest directly an index.

2. A mathematical structure that gives enhanced compounding to accumulators, and the avoidance of negative compounding for withdrawers.

Those benefits are evergreen and timeless, yet in real time periods have proven to be a better total return proposition (with lower volatility) than various peers.

After reading this book, if you are unconvinced of the argument for dividend growth going forward, I will have no beef with you. Just make sure your argument is not based on a fallacious understanding of the past.

Mr. Utility wants credit for his defeat of Mr. Nasdaq! And Mr. Income certainly wants credit for carrying Mr. Utility across the finish line.

# 7

## THE THREAT OF INFLATION

### The Self-Contained Offense and Defense in Dividend Growth Stocks

*"Inflation is when you pay fifteen dollars for the ten-dollar haircut you used to get for five dollars when you had hair."*

—SAM EWING

*"I do not think it is an exaggeration to say that history is largely a history of inflation, usually inflations engineered by governments for the gain of governments."*

—F.A. HAYEK

There is an enemy working against investors more insidious than any other we often discuss. Indeed, the fact that we rarely discuss this is a big part of why it is so insidious. Investors tend to focus heavily on the various risks that they can see or that manifest themselves dramatically and frequently. But this enemy does not provide such visibility or provoke such efficacious focus. I refer to the deterioration of purchasing power caused by the forces of inflation.

Just as the danger of getting a sunburn is enhanced when there is cloud cover because sunbathers tend to let their guard down, inflation is a formidable foe to investors because it is invisible, slow-moving, and does its damage over time, not in a given monthly statement.

When politicians say, "we need to take 30% of your income," they assess income taxes and people have to pay all in one year. Voters hate it and work to minimize their tax liability. Raise taxes too much and voters throw politicians out of office.

But not so with inflation. In this instance, a politician can easily take 30% of a person's money, if not more—as long as they do it 2–3% at a time, over a twenty-year period, voters tend to let it go. Investors tend to ignore it. Citizens tend to not see it. But in what sense is inflation just as confiscatory and damaging as an immediate tax?

It detracts from the wealth and quality of life of people.

Investors ignore inflation to their own peril. To fully appreciate how seriously I take this, you must go back to my epiphany described in Chapter 1. All investing is done for the purpose of returning a greater amount of cash in the future. Whether that be for a future generation (your grandkids), or for a third-party beneficiary (your church), or for your own retirement, and whether it be over time (periodic cash distributions) or via a lump-sum withdrawal (your daughter's wedding expenses), money goes into an investment vehicle for the purpose of cash coming out.

But it should go without saying that if the cash coming back out in the future is inadequate to cover what the money would have covered when it went in, something has failed.

Consider two scenarios:

1. An investor socks away $20,000 to buy a boat in five years. The boat costs $20,000 now. At the end of five years, the portfolio has declined 10% (to $18,000), and the boat still costs $20,000. That investor is 10% short.

2. An investor socks away $20,000 to buy a boat in five years. The boat costs $20,000 now. At the end of five years, the portfolio has increased 5% to $21,000 (no decrease in value), but the boat now costs $23,000 due to inflation. That investor is 10% short.

Which investor is better off in these two scenarios? The answer is, of course, neither. The objective was to buy a boat in five years. One is short due to poor investing performance. The other is short due to the reality of moderate inflation. They are short by the same amount, but for different reasons. Comparing the two nominal amounts of money is futile. In all practical senses, the real-life objective of a boat purchase is unsuccessful in both of these scenarios.

There are infinite illustrations available to make a point that should be painfully clear to everyone. *The real definition of "money" is purchasing power.*

As we state in our core principles at The Bahnsen Group,[29] "currency is not money; it is a product used to exchange money. The objective of investing is not to create or preserve a fixed dollar amount; it is to facilitate the adequate ability to purchase what one wants with their funds. Therefore, to ignore inflation in defining risk is financial malpractice."

Nominal returns are trumped by real returns for the person who will use the future money. Real returns are simply the nominal returns less the impact of inflation. A 7% nominal return with 2% inflation (a 5% real return) is far superior in the real world to an 8% nominal return with 4% inflation (a 4% real return).

Of course, when comparing investments, we do not have the option to alter the inflation expectation. An inflation environment of 3% does not become an inflation environment of 2% just because we switched investment strategies. In other words, inflation is going to be what it is going to be. We cannot control the inflation rate; we can only control the investment approach we take to defend against it.

What creates inflation? And while we are on the subject, what is inflation? Economists have disagreed about the answers to both of these questions for decades upon decades, yet I will share what I have found the most convincing answer to be, by far.

Milton Friedman famously said inflation is "too much money chasing too few goods." The elegance of this statement is found in both elements of the compound. On one hand, "too much money" refers to excessive amounts of money supply put into circulation in the economy. And on the other hand, "too few goods" refers to the level of production of goods and services in the economy. An economy with growing goods and services needs more money in circulation to facilitate the exchange of goods and services. When the money supply and economic output level get out of equilibrium, the result is either inflation or deflation (depending on the direction).

Is the mere existence of additional money supply the same as inflation? In fact, the money stock has to be multiplied by the velocity of itself to determine the price level in an economy. Money supply leads to higher prices (inflation) when that money is circulating in the economy. A slowdown in economic activity leads to a decline in circulation of money, and therefore the stock of money does not lead to higher inflation, per se.

Irving Fisher's quantity theory of money is:

$$MV = PT$$

*where **M** represents the stock of money,*
***V** represents the velocity (or circulation) of money*
*in the economy,*
***P** equals the price level, and*
***T** equals the volume of transactions*

I have avoided such dry economic academia in this book on purpose, but am providing this simple theory of money and prices to explain why inflation so often confounds people. Since 2009, many have been stunned by the failure of their forecasts for hyperinflation to surface, not understanding that the V in the above equation has been low enough to keep the P down.

Another thing that makes inflation tough to understand is how tough it is to measure. The price level (P)—the combined level of prices across all goods and services in an economy—is not something readily available to us. And for the last twenty to twenty-five years, significant deflationary forces (of a positive variety) have been at play, primarily in the technology arena. We talk a lot about an ice cream cone that cost $0.15 decades ago costing $3 now, yet we don't always remember that a VCR cost $600 in 1985, whereas a blu-ray/DVD player costs $30 now. Additionally, there is a "value-added" component that makes inflation very tough to measure. Does anyone think comparing the first-generation cell phones to an iPhone X is a good apples-to-apples comparison? In other words, the product we are contrasting prices to is often a different product altogether due to technological innovations and advancements.

As an economist, I contrast the subject of inflation in an aca-demic macroeconomic context from the more practical setting of financial planning. If a family is going to the grocery store today for bread, milk, and fruit, and they spend X, inflation should be understood in a practical sense as the increase in X from today to a future point in time. Therefore, an investor, in planning their defense against inflation, would be wise to consider what their spending targets will really be. Not all inflation is created equal.

This simply means that society-wide measurements of infla-tion are very difficult because there are highly different rates of inflation in different targets of our spending. (See Figure 7–1.) An individual needing to spend money in the future on a

**FIGURE 7–1**

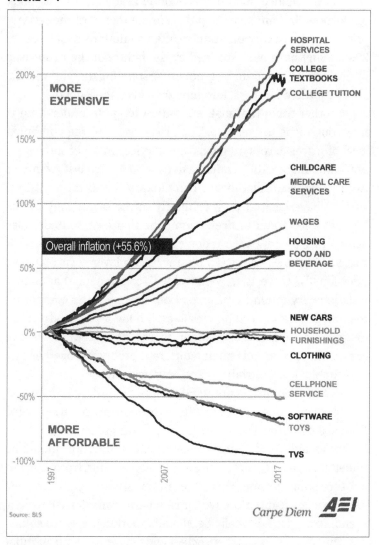

home purchase, a college education, and health care[30] will likely have very different inflation planning needs than one who has paid for their kids' college education already, owns their home free and clear, and has an employer paying the full cost of their health insurance.

All of this is to say that inflation is complicated, often misunderstood, and frequently ignored. Those who do not ignore it, but do misunderstand it, will often misdiagnose it, and have often made the compound error of wrongly prescribing a solution. Most notorious in these inflation-defenses has been the idea of gold as the desired hedge. Some historical perspective is in order.

The 1970s were the last period of really dramatic inflation in the United States (with a spillover into the early 1980s). The Nixon administration's steps to weaken the dollar combined with a decade of weak economic growth and stagnating taxes and regulation left Americans disgusted by the double whammy of inflation. Incentives were very low to invest in new projects, knowing their profit potential would be compressed by the impact of inflation by the time the project was completed. Costs were high and rising; interest rates were high and rising because of the high inflation in the economy; and economic growth and productivity were wholly inadequate. As Americans longed for protection against 1970s inflation, an entire cottage-industry came to be, promoting gold ownership as the panacea for the insidious effects of inflation. And as is often the case, gold became en vogue as the inflation elixir of choice, just in time for it to completely fail to be so.

From 1980 to 2001, the inflation-adjusted value of gold fell by over 80%. The consumer price index (CPI) in that same period doubled.[31] (See Figure 7–2.) Gold certainly had a large move to the upside from 2001 to 2011, but from 1980 through present date, gold is down over 32% when adjusted for inflation, or over 1% *per year.*

**FIGURE 7–2**

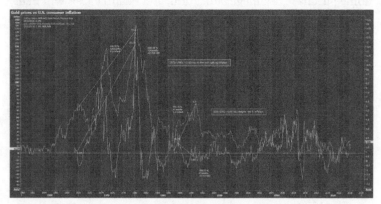

Gold prices vs. U.S. consumer inflation, *Reuters*, March 1, 2018.

One would think that thirty-eight years is an adequate time period for a long-term investor to gauge the impact of inflation on a popular and common inflation hedge.

Gold may very well offer various characteristics that some investors find appealing. Even if it has not been an effective defense against moderate inflation, it may very well provide "crisis hedge" benefits (though certain crises may disagree with that as well). Gold may offer a benefit to investors seeking an "alternate currency," but even then it has to be bought with a certain currency, so it is still denominated in the currency it is bought and then sold in.

You will misread my comments on gold if you take them to mean that I believe gold is going to go lower in price in the future. I make no forecast on such a thing (and I would be very wary of anyone you read who does offer such a forecast). Gold may go up in the future, and it may go down, but my comment addresses something far more knowable and easily verifiable: historically, gold has not been a great hedge against moderate inflation, period.

There is a type of sociology and, certainly, a high degree of marketability that has helped to formulate a narrative around gold ownership. People loving feeling prepared for disasters, and they certainly love *sounding* like they are prepared. Fearmongering newsletters and commercials that sell anxiety around threats and catastrophes do not need to provide historical data or empirical support for the conclusions that they offer; indeed, their conclusion is rather transparent, "buy something [gold] from me!" Sales pitches are not expected to be thorough economic analysis, let alone rooted in objectivity. And the actual logistics of how gold will be practically monetized to offset the impact of inflation is certainly not discussed!

So let's talk about dividend growth and inflation, because I do take the threat of inflation seriously, even if I find it important for people to appreciate the velocity of money, recognize the disparate impact of inflation on different goods and services, and find gold to be a poor inflation hedge over the last forty years. What I do find important is the damage done to my client's purchasing power over long periods of time by even modest levels of inflation.[32] (See Figure 7–3.)

A 3% inflation level eats away almost half of one's purchasing power in just twenty years. Maybe inflation will only be 2%, and maybe your timeline is even less than 20 years, but, even then, some management of that inflation impact is crucial. As discussed at the beginning of this chapter, the common tendency is to ignore inflation's impact because it is not striking, immediate, or dramatic. Dividend growth investing represents a very time-tested defense against that slow-drip danger.

The first point I will make about dividend growth is that its very structure allows for an investor to keep up with inflation. The "inflation" we are talking about now in a practical sense is "rising prices." A constant income does not do much to keep up with rising prices. But where can an investor see their income

**FIGURE 7–3**

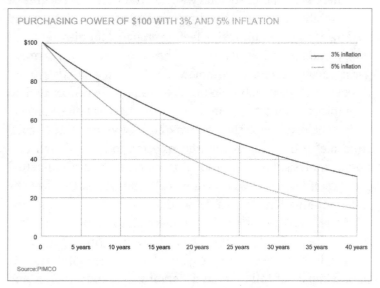

PURCHASING POWER OF $100 WITH 3% AND 5% INFLATION

Source:PIMCO

grow, without having to raid the principal of the investment paying the growing income? With stocks that increase their distributions to investors, of course.

If inflation is an increase in the price level of society, it can also be said that price increases in cheeseburgers, soda pop, your electric bill, diapers, toothpaste, a shopping mall tenant's rent, and your phone bill are, well, "inflation." And if those prices are going higher, it is because the company passed on the impact of inflation to their customers! Shareholders see their revenues rise in concert with higher prices, enabling dividends to grow in concert with the same. Of course, it is not always this simple—companies must maintain pricing power and manage their profit margins effectively. But the very definition of inflation means that companies are passing along the impact, and shareholders can see their economic distributions inflate with the prices in question!

Another way to put it is that if there is no revenue increase at a company level, there likely is not inflation (the inverse is not necessarily true, by the way; you can have a revenue increase without inflation due to innovation, competition, and other factors). That revenue increase may not be profitable right away, as inflationary effects may be eating into profit margins, but again, pricing power and effective management lead to an extraordinary weapon against this dynamic.

The fact that there is a lag effect between price increases and company profits does not negate the point I am making, it reinforces it! The complexity of price volatility, currency exchange rates, and profit margins begs for talented managers and operators. A static bond portfolio provides no opportunity to manage around this impact. Revenues, profits, and distributions from profit (dividends) all inflate with inflation. There is a real internal rate of return that can be used to counteract the impact of inflation.

Mechanics mean everything, once again, and it is the growing income of dividend growth stocks that provides *practical* significance to investors. Then it is *economic logic* that allows asset prices to sustain and grow as well-run companies offset the impact of inflation to their businesses.

The mechanics of these moving parts are illustrated in Figure 7–4. Dividend growth offsets the impact of inflation, and then some; constant income stays flat without considering inflation and declines substantially when inflation is factored in:

Historically, rising inflation means higher interest rates. Consider the relative performance of dividend growers in periods of rising rates in Figure 7–5.

This defensiveness is an undeniable benefit of dividend growth investing. Investors who fear the impact of inflation have a time-tested weapon against it, combative in both its economics and mechanics. We have lived in a prolonged era of low interest

**FIGURE 7–4**

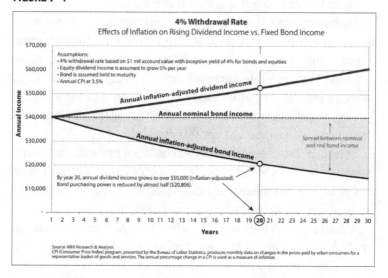

**FIGURE 7–5**

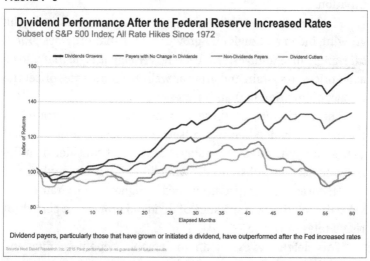

rates since the financial crisis. It is not the subject of this book as to whether or not those low rates will persist, or will move modestly or meaningfully higher. But to the extent that rising rates represent some risk in one's investment portfolio, dividend growth is yet again a proven antidote to such a development.

Through all of the misunderstandings about the causes of inflation, the realities of inflation, and the flawed antidotes to inflation, my purpose has been to propose for you *the best inflation-fighter I have ever seen: The dividends you receive from well-run companies, themselves growing at a rate multiples of the inflation rate itself.*

# 8

## BUT WHAT ABOUT STOCK BUYBACKS?

*"You don't compare buybacks, a balance sheet transaction, to the income statement.... One is allowed to think buybacks are a bad idea, or being executed worse than before, without the crazy stuff."*

—CLIFFORD ASNESS

One of the most difficult situations is to face making an argument where your conclusion is agreeable for a lot of people, but for entirely different reasons than the ones those people are using. I have often said, both in one's methodology of investing and in other ideological aspects of life, that I prefer people share my premises than my conclusions. Of course, getting to the right place, for the right reasons, is preferred. But sometimes one may simply draw a different conclusion than another would from the same tenets, beliefs, and assumptions. That isn't ideal, I suppose, but it allows for a constructive conversation when there is already common ground. It is easier to realign one's interpretation of data than it is to fully reconstruct what data matters, why it matters, what the objective is, and so forth.

To summarize, I believe the ideal scenario when it comes to formulating a coherent investment philosophy is:

1. Right premises, right conclusions.

*And second best to that is:*

**2.** Right premises, wrong conclusions.

*With there being a big danger that lurks when there is:*

**3.** Wrong premises, a right conclusion.

*And of course, the worst framework of all:*

**4.** Wrong premises, wrong conclusions.

It should be pointed out that number three always leads to number four, eventually. A framework filled with inaccurate understandings of capital markets and fallacious commitments is not capable of delivering consistently right outcomes. We teach foundational truisms—*first things* or *first principles*—when it comes to one's view of ethics, civics, morality, theology, of so many disciplines—because we understand that the base of intellectual ingredients we use will have everything to do with the final product.

The world of investing is no different. If one believes that hocus-pocus on a chart tells them where a stock price is headed (it doesn't) and they end up accurately forecasting a given outcome, the conclusion did not validate the premise. In fact, it may increase the risk around that individual's investing perspective, because their accurate conclusion may have emboldened them for future forecasts while the flawed premises persist. There are key principles that matter in investing that, when upheld consistently and cogently, lead to successful investing outcomes. Likewise, there are destructive principles that, when acted upon, lead (eventually) to disaster. If one believes that the market can be "timed," all failures of outcome can be blamed on the execution of the premise instead of the wrong belief itself. But when one accepts the impossibility of successfully "timing" the market, there is no need to turn knobs on how to "do it better." The right belief system eliminates the need to try.

We could spend a lot of time on what represents cogent foundational principles in investing and what does not. Worldviews are built off of assumptions and guiding beliefs that are subject to scrutiny, to consistency, and to time. I do believe there are a lot of mistaken presuppositions floating around the world of financial markets, but, generally, the destructive conclusions that inevitably come invalidate such theories rather quickly and there is no need to fret any further.

My rationale for this long set-up is that I am about to present a chapter where the conclusion will have some degree of negativity associated with it about stock buybacks. I am not against stock buybacks, per se, but I am going to argue for the superiority of dividend payments when it comes to shareholder-friendly uses of free cash flow. I am also going to point out some of the non-ideal motives that exist in authorizations of stock buybacks. Most importantly, I am going to argue for the pragmatic benefits of growing dividend payments versus the benefits for shareholders in stock buybacks, mechanically and otherwise. Taken together, a reader could very well conclude that I am "anti-stock buybacks."

The fact of the matter is I am not anti-stock-buybacks. They play a pivotal role in capital markets in our country, have plenty of potentially very shareholder-friendly purposes, and are a vital tool in the corporate treasurer's modern finance toolbox. So I am pro-share-repurchases, even if I will spend most of my time in this chapter contrasting them to what I consider to be a superior option for shareholders: paying an increasing dividend to them.

Here is where premises and conclusions are important— even where I am negative or wary around stock buybacks, the conclusions come from an entirely and categorically different place than the mania surrounding stock buybacks today. There is currently a significant movement driven by wrong and faulty premises and, in some cases, it may sound like there is occasional overlap between my view on certain things and this anti-buyback movement's view of things. There isn't any overlap. You would think I would welcome any comers who draw the same conclusions I do, but I do not. It is that first category above I am after: right premises, right conclusions. And in the case of many contemporary critics of stock buybacks, there is a "derangement syndrome" at play from which I am eager to be separated. So I proceed with caution, determined to offer a cogent presentation on dividend growth, and yet zealous to avoid making bad arguments to find a good conclusion.

What is behind the bad arguments for opposing share buybacks? Most criticisms of share buybacks are really criticisms of private ownership of capital and rooted in a disproven view of capital versus labor (though with varying degrees of self-awareness around their own intellectual commitments). Essentially, the current hysteria around share buybacks seems rooted in deep misunderstandings of how share buybacks work, why they exist, and what benefits they do provide. Up against *these* criticisms, it is imperative that share buybacks actually be *defended*. There will be legitimate basis for critique and to argue for the superiority from an investment standpoint of dividend growth in a moment, but for now, let me wear the other hat as I want to get the premises right.

The critique you most often hear is that share buybacks suppress wages. It is false, but it carries a powerful rhetorical advantage to it—we as a society want people to see their wages grow, so, naturally, it comes with a built-in emotional advantage to state wages for hard-working families suffer because of stock buybacks.

Cliff Asness, the guru of mathematical investing and quantitative genius who founded AQR Capital Management, has published much on stock buybacks, including his quote from the opening of this chapter. He has also asked, "Is there any financial topic that people say more silly things about than buybacks?" Asness is correct, and unfortunately, the current stock-buyback debate is more than a simple disagreement between billionaire portfolio managers. Underneath the gross misperceptions of those opposing buybacks is a dangerous ideology whose message is gaining traction with an unsuspecting audience.

To complain that buybacks use up money that could be spent on other company expenses like wages and bonuses is essentially to argue against profits themselves because buybacks are paid for from the cash generated from a company's profits. Fundamentally, this view suffers from classic zero-sum fallacy: the idea that stock buybacks are "pulling money away from employee compensation, research and development, and other corporate priorities—with potentially sweeping effects on business dynamism, income and wealth inequality, working-class economic stagnation, and the country's growth rate."[33]

Blaming buybacks for sluggish economic growth, low productivity, and piddling increases in worker compensation is a political argument, not an investment one, but it is flawed on both fronts. Complaining that "companies are working overtime to make their owners richer in the short term, more so than to improve their longer-term competitiveness or to invest in their workers"[34] is old-fashioned class envy—both morally and economically flawed. It also is not an investment argument one way or the other.

It's important to understand where the cash that funds buybacks comes from, what they are used for, and what exactly they do to a company's balance sheet. Buybacks are not a company expense; they are a use of cash from company profits: from the money that remains after expenses are deducted from revenue. So, a company can be criticized for pocketing profits that could be spent on expenses such as research and development or for using its profits to buy back shares rather than paying them out in dividends or saving them for the future. But share buybacks are not a competitor to other company expenses—to argue otherwise is ignorant at best, and dishonest at worst.

The argument alleging a crowding out of wage growth created by stock buybacks borrows heavily on the claim that workers could have been paid more in a world of fewer stock buybacks. There is a mathematical truth to the argument that more wages could mean less profits and less profits could mean more wages. It is also unhelpful to the present discussion. The question ought to be: What drives value for the stakeholders of the company, building the incentive to create jobs, grow wages, and increase economic productivity that serves as the engine of free enterprise? Attacks on profits themselves, if successful, shrink the pool of money from which wages are paid out.

Indeed, stock buybacks happen to be the very source of tremendous wage growth for employees. The effect of stock grants to employees over the last twenty years has been unprecedented balance-sheet wealth for mid-level programmers, administrators, salespeople, designers, and others. Try convincing employees of Apple that their annual stock grants do not count as wage growth! Where do the shares of stock come from that are used in restricted-stock grants and stock-option plans? From shares the company has purchased in buybacks!

The objection to stock buybacks in the name of defending laborers is an objection against capital formation, a false dilemma at its root. For if one believes that stock buybacks are made at the expense of research, opportunistic acquisitions, training, equipment, and worker wages, then one believes that those driving stock buybacks are seeking to undermine the very profits that pay for them.

The idea that share buybacks starve access to new investment is absurd on its face. A company balance sheet with more equity (higher earnings-per-share) has that much more buying power and that much more borrowing power in the open market. Investors will seek the most efficient capital allocation they can find, and companies seeking to attract new investment will respond to that pursuit. Again, no real-life assessment could ever conclude that companies generating growing profits and using said cash flow to reduce share count (value creation) are cutting off their access to purchasing power. That binary thinking lacks awareness of balance-sheet management and profit-and-loss management.

As the very subject of this book obviously indicates, I find dividends to be a more investor-friendly way to reward shareholders, giving them positive cash flow and allowing them to realize monetization of their investment periodically, as opposed to constantly compounding the risk of a given holding. But that is an argument for how a corporate board should allocate the capital the company has generated via company profits, not an argument against profits themselves.

I hope I have adequately persuaded you that my "issues" with stock buybacks do not come from the same place as predominant arguments against stock buybacks. The debate for us as investors is entirely about what to do with profits once they are achieved, not whether or not profits themselves are healthy in a free society.

A publicly traded company has several options for what to do with their "profits." We, as shareholders, have a lot of interest in what company management elects to do because the entire objective of being an equity investor is to receive a "claim on a company's profits." That "claim," though, does not inherently speak to the manifestation of the claim! Company management gets to select and implement the use of such profits. The options, in no particular order, include the following:

1. **Reinvest in the company.** A company generates revenue, pays expenses, has profit left, and uses that profit to create a new product, expand into a new market, or pursue a new avenue of business success. This is a very common use of profits and a perfectly legitimate one, in theory.

2. **Pay down debt.** A company that has debt on its balance sheet has only two ways to pay it down: from a balance sheet transaction or from profits earned. In other words, one can replace debt by issuing equity (balance sheet) or they can borrow new money to replace old debt (balance sheet). And other than that, the only way to reduce debt is to pay it from actual profits earned. One could argue that the primary reason to issue debt is the earnings that will eventually be generated off of the activity that the debt enabled.

3. **Mergers and Acquisitions (M&A).** A less common but still profound option for company earnings is to utilize profits to buy another company that may serve a strategic purpose: for example, to eliminate competition, create more operational scale, or find cost synergies. Sometimes profits "rolled" into buying other companies can help (or not) create even bigger profits in the future.

4. **Cash Retention.** This is a "rainy day fund" and simply means that a company retains its earnings, pays taxes on them, and holds greater cash on their balance sheet, presumably for a future use.

5. **Stock Buybacks.** This is, of course, the subject of this chapter. This dominant use of cash from profits creates a higher "earnings per share" as there are less shares to have a claim on the same level of earnings. A huge

advantage to this approach is capacity—there is a seemingly (not literally) infinite amount of shares outstanding for a large publicly traded corporation, and so it enables a treasurer to put a lot of money to work at once. As we will see in a moment, it also enables a lot of the compensation programs that are very common in the modern economy.

6. **Dividend Payments.** And then, of course, the subject of this whole book. In its simplest form, a dividend is just a portion of the profits the company earned paid out to the shareholders—the cleanest and easiest-to-define manifestation of a "claim on earnings."

It is far outside the scope of this chapter to unpack all the complexity that goes into what a company does with their after-tax earnings. CFOs do not pick one item from the aforementioned list and throw all the profits at that one item. There is always a multiplicity of elections that are intended to juxtapose the company's long-term growth objectives, optimal balance sheet needs, demands from credit agencies, and specific business model. It is one of the reasons press coverage of "stock buybacks" versus "dividend payments" is so pedestrian—a massive amount of stock buybacks are literally just done for purposes of funding stock to employees through various employee compensation programs. Some companies are aggressive in these programs (Silicon Valley generally is) and some have no such propensity. The specific needs and complexities of each company warrant very different capital distribution programs.

I, therefore, acknowledge that one company's split between share buybacks and dividend distributions may very appropriately be different from another company's split between the same. But a newer criticism of dividend payments is that share buybacks represent a more tax-efficient way to return cash to shareholders. It is often a thoughtful argument and it certainly warrants some discussion. Do shareholders receive the same economic benefits that they would from dividends through share buybacks? My fervent response is that no, they do not.

I am going to structure my response to this claim—that share buybacks are just as good as dividend payments for the investor, only with better tax ramifications—into four categories:

1. Compounding of risk
2. Alignment of interests
3. Mechanics of cash flow
4. Volatility of outcome

"Compounding of risk" is first because I do believe it is the most important category. Fundamentally, a share buyback at the corporate level is not a return of cash to the shareholder and, as we discussed in Chapter 1, all investors care about is the receipt of cash (either now, or later; either in big chunks, or small ones). I concede that a share buyback makes the underlying value higher, but it does not monetize the investment.

Assume a company makes $10,000 of profits, and has a hundred shareholders who own one hundred shares each. If the company takes that $10,000 of profits, and buys back one hundred shares of stock, it now has ninety-nine shareholders. Ninety-nine shareholders now own something that has the same value that a hundred shareholders previously owned. It is antidilutive; it gives people more ownership in something.

But that "something" is a business, with risk. That is perfectly okay—that is, of course, what a shareholder signed up for. But they agreed to take on risk to get a certain return on that risk. With dividends, I would humbly suggest, they receive a monetization on that return, justifying the risk, over and over and over. Should something go wrong with the company later—the advent of a viable competitor, mistakes out of the management suite, a scandal, an obsolete product or service—that shareholder will always have the dividends they received. They monetized their investment. They were paid for the risk. The company has less cash, because it paid it to shareholders, but the shareholder has cash. They got paid. They received a reward for their investment. And this process of being compensated for risk takes place for the dividend investor, quarter over quarter, over and over again, throughout one's time in the investment (assuming the company continues to pay it).

With the stock buyback, the shareholder does not receive cash, and does not receive shares. There is no visible contribution into their ledger, so to speak. That does not mean it is not a benefit for, as I said, the shares they own now have a claim on more earnings, because there are less shares than there previously were. But by continuing to invest with no payoff to the investor, what the investor is doing is compounding their risk. Each year that the company buys more shares, the company has simply asked the shareholders to defer their monetization. The company may be getting more profitable, and those buybacks are accretive for the investor, but they are allowing uncompensated risk to build.

Now, to further complicate things, often share buybacks are not even reducing the share count or increasing earnings-per-share to the investor in any meaningful way. They are, instead, a compensation mechanism to fund stock options, restrict stock issuance, and other such executive compensation programs. You could argue, of course, that this is money the company would have to pay to these given employees, managers, and executives, so by issuing stock this way (with shares purchased by the company via buybacks) they are protecting profits by limiting what otherwise would be an increase in wages and bonuses. This is certainly true, in theory, but all that means is that the investor is being confused by what the actual profits were, and the actual amount of cash he or she has a claim on. To refer to shares bought back by the company as a "return of cash to shareholders" when what it really represents is using the balance sheet to alter the income statement, is somewhat disingenuous.

Another complicating factor are the potential conflicts of interest in the C-suite. So many companies compensate their CEO and CFO off of earnings-per-share metrics and stock performance metrics that a strong and real conflict exists between sustainable growth and long-term financial health (the type dividends reinforce) versus shorter term optics that may disproportionately benefit those making the call (such as stock buybacks).

Do stock buybacks signal the same thing to the market that dividends do—that company executives believe the stock is under-valued? If so, they are not very good at such a valuation decision! Stock buybacks perennially peak at times of market highs and decline at times of market lows. Company executives are no better market timers than any of the rest of us! Consistent cash flow growth paid out through responsible dividend payments is measurable, definable, and rules-based. Heavy stock buybacks can mean a lot of things, and be a lot of things, and some of those things are good, but it has no historical precedent of meaning that the company is actually under-valued.

Many critics of stock buybacks cherry-pick companies that bought back excessive amounts of stock and subsequently saw their share prices decline, to make an argument against stock buybacks. Again, I have to separate myself from that line of argument. General Electric and IBM have struggled over the last twenty years (GE a lot more than IBM), and they have spent a lot of money on stock buybacks, but they have spent a lot of money on dividends, too! My academic integrity is too high to cherry-pick certain examples of a thesis I hold to and try and make

**FIGURE 8–1**

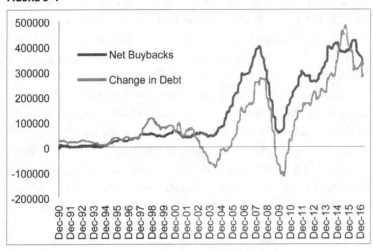

SG Cross Asset Research/Equity Quant, Heisenberg Report, February 20, 2018.

it normative, or try and pretend the same thing can't be done in my own methodology.

But one legitimate point critics make about share buybacks is that they are often funded with more debt. Indeed, the correlation between debt issuance and share buybacks is rather surreal. (See Figure 8–1.)

Once again, a potential rebuttal here may be, "but companies sometimes issue debt to pay the dividends, too!" Fortunately, I answer that one comprehensively in our next chapter. My point in bringing up the debt funding of share buybacks is that they are presented as a mere use of cash flow (to compensate the shareholder without incurring a tax consequence), by improving the balance sheet (more proportionate ownership of the equity). And in reality, the equity that gets more valuable on an earnings-per-share basis often has more debt next to it in the capital structure, further intensifying that compounding of risk for the equity shareholder.

The solution to excessive debt funding of share buybacks is to have a natural interest rate in the economy, not one artificially below the return on invested capital. Monetary policy since 2008 has incentivized this financial maneuvering, and one must rely on wisdom in the treasury department of the company to manage this potential behavior.

And finally, as far as peripheral circumstances that also create a misalignment of interest, companies do not "declare" a buyback the way they declare a dividend. A dividend is approved, declared, and paid as a matter of process. Share buybacks are "authorized," but then very sporadically administered, with little or no transparency to shareholders as to when or for how much. They are not obligatory; companies can authorize but not execute buybacks at will. One would assume that a company has a good reason to not complete a share buyback authorization, but the point is that the only optics to the shareholder in advance of the capital activity is the authorization amount. They must wait until the next quarter to know what actually got done! Dividends provide actual transparency by eliminating this delta between intent and reality.

But aside from the compounding of risk perpetual buybacks without dividends represent, and the potential misalignment of interests between management and shareholders, there also is a basic mechanical issue at play. *Investors cannot eat share buybacks!* Back to the withdrawal issues of Chapter 5, no matter what one believes about the efficacy of share buybacks in maximizing shareholder value, they do not create functional liquidity for the investors who desire periodic cash flow. An investor whose portfolio is entirely driven by companies "returning cash" by not returning cash would have to sell shares to monetize their investment, essentially creating the exact same mechanical risk we discussed in that earlier chapter.

**FIGURE 8–2**

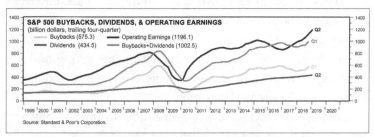

That mechanical risk is not to be taken lightly, as we previously covered. But even it fails to properly demonstrate the magnitude of this contrast.

Dividends tend to be far, far more stable than share buybacks. (See Figure 8–2.) This reality, validated through history in convincing fashion when being discussed in the context of faithful dividend growers, sets a tradition and expectation. Market expectations for dividend payers and dividend growers is that they will pay and that they will grow. No such expectation exists for "buybacks," even though periods of decline are probably the best time to be buying back shares! Instead, it creates a cyclicality effect that places the buyback activity heavily in line with the stock price and the earnings. Of course, some investors may welcome this volatility relationship, but the investor looking for a more stable experience will find dividends to be more reliable, even avoiding negative movement at all (in terms of the return of cash to shareholders).

In conclusion, stock buybacks are a valuable use of after-tax earnings in many situations. They do not represent a threat to wages, workers, and innovation, as profits themselves drive all growth incentives and make possible the very wages and workers that we are concerned about. A company can be poorly run, but the profit motive is a healthy one to drive innovation and productivity.

It is what a company does with those profits that is our concern. History has been clear that a heavy emphasis on dividend distributions to shareholders creates more alignment with shareholders than stock buybacks do, is less susceptible to manipulation, is less cyclical and unreliable, and is more mechanically beneficial to most investors.

I believe the conclusion to be right here, and more importantly, I believe it to be rooted in the right premises and thinking. Let that be our objective in all considerations.

# 9

# TO THIS END WE WORK
## Avoiding Dividend Cuts

*"Investing would be so much simpler if investors were focused on this simple compound question, and nothing else: Is this dividend safe, and will it grow?"*

—LOWELL MILLER

There is a vulnerability to this book's central thesis that simply must be addressed: the risk of declining dividend income for an investor. Put differently, what happens if the companies a dividend growth investor owns begin to cut their dividend?

I have demonstrated that fluctuating asset prices are not a vulnerability as long as the income is sustained and rising. That negation of equity price risk is fully dependent on a dividend that lasts.

I have argued that a growing dividend can be a sign of a more stable company. This is rather unhelpful but for the presumption of the growing dividend; for indeed, we believe a company growing its dividend is more stable—but therefore, that benefit of enhanced portfolio stability is undermined by a declining dividend!

I have made the case that the mechanics of reinvesting dividends provide a "compounding within compounding" dynamic in which market volatility enhances our returns and creates a long-term cash flow that is exponentially higher than it otherwise would be. What eliminates reinvestment? The elimination of the dividend. What reduces the compounding argument? The reduction of the dividend.

I have described the incredible peace of mind that a withdrawer can have when they know their income will be there, regardless of portfolio pricing. Asset prices will go up and down, but the reliability of the income (let alone its growth) insulates a retiree, or other withdrawer, from market volatility. But if the income declines? The system is turned on its head!

I have established the performance premium that well-managed dividend growth portfolios offer over time. But, of course, if you eliminate the dividend from that argument, you eliminate the argument for a performance premium.

I have shown how a portfolio that grows its income over time provides a phenomenal hedge and defense against destructive inflation. A loss of purchasing power *is* a loss of value, and when expenses are growing faster than one's income, the investor is losing even if the statement doesn't show it in principal "value." So, an income from a portfolio growing in excess of the inflation rate remedies this concern, but if that income growth becomes jeopardized, the entire argument is clearly jeopardized.

*Using package delivery company UPS, you see here that UPS's stock price has endured completely normal price volatility over the last five years on multiple occasions, and yet its dividend payment has remained rock steady reliable, with sustained, consistent growth. The result is a growing dividend and a stock price that have continued to advance.* (See Figure 9–1.)

I make the argument for dividend growth investing while being transparent about this rather obvious fact:

*The various arguments in support of dividend growth investing you have read in this book presuppose that the dividend income in one's portfolio is, in fact, growing.*

**FIGURE 9–1**

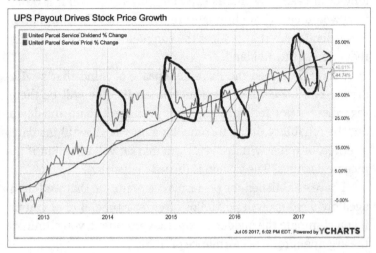

This vulnerability, however, represents no threat to the central tenet of the book, for the sustainability of a portfolio's dividend growth is indeed something that can be protected. We can be aware of the existential damage dividend reductions *would* represent, all the while managing toward a portfolio free of dividend cuts. The work that entails is the subject of this chapter.

Before we delve into what matters for avoiding dividend cuts in individual securities, let's separate that from the subject of *portfolio* income. Put differently, do all of the strategy merits and arguments die if *one company* cuts its dividend, or does it take a portfolio-wide reduction of income to actually undermine the strategy thesis? The answer is, of course, that it is cash flow creation out of an entire portfolio that matters, not merely from one individual stock. And yet, a portfolio with *a stock* that cuts its dividend could be a portfolio with *several stocks* that cut their dividend. And a portfolio with several stocks that cut their dividend could easily become a portfolio of declining income. In other words, diversification matters, it helps, and it should not be taken lightly; but, it also cannot be assumed to be a fully self-sufficient defense against the danger of dividend reduction. A portfolio managed to allow any dividend cut is potentially vulnerable.

All things being equal, in periods where certain dividend cuts are possible (generally periods of economic contraction), it behooves investors to have that diversification benefit working for them. My belief is that there are *economic* characteristics and *cultural* propensities that give us the ability to construct a portfolio *highly likely* to not experience dividend cuts. Can a name or two within a well-designed portfolio built around these economic and cultural realities still experience an unexpected dividend cut? Sure, in theory, it can happen. But do we have overwhelming empirical evidence to suggest that, even in the case of individual outlier dividend cuts, this portfolio orientation (in aggregate) can be well-insulated from income reduction?

The fact of the matter is that it would be hard to envision a more ripe threat to dividend sustainability than the 2000–2010 period, bookended by two nasty recessions (the second of which is graciously referred to as "The Great Recession"). What held together dividend income (and dividend growth-of-income) during this decade was not cherry-picked portfolio performance, but rather, a deep inclination across a wide array of stocks in different categories focused on cash flow stability. (See Figure 9–2.) If the opening act of this century—a 40%+ drop in equity index values, and the worst terrorist attack on American soil in history—could not undermine the aggregate dividend growth of well-diversified, properly-selected dividend-growing companies, shouldn't that be worth some degree of confidence? And if the worst financial recession since the Great Depression—where significant financial sector stocks were, in fact, cutting their dividends—did not spoil the thesis, shouldn't that embolden our belief in this concept?

**FIGURE 9–2**

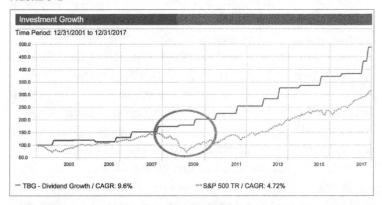

FactSet Research, January 2018. The dividend growth model uses a basket of 30+ dividend stocks presently owned and back-tested to 2001 for how composite dividend growth performed. The income grew at 9.6% per year with no annual declines in composite dividend income. The yellow line represents the price-only performance of the S&P 500 over this period (2002–2017).[35] This is a hypothetical portfolio constructed for illustration, with no attempt to screen out dividend cutters.

The purpose of this chapter is not merely to reinforce the historical success of dividend growth-oriented stocks during periods of market distress. Past performance is no guarantee of future results. Rather, it is to demonstrate *how* past performance has enabled dividend sustainability, and *what* is needed to maintain it. Dividend growth is not index-able, at least not with the same degree of confidence that we are assuming in this chapter. To index dividend growth is to assume past characteristics are maintained in the future. The characteristics that made past dividend growers what they were have to be managed, maintained, and monitored through time.

How do we avoid the companies that cut their dividends? Dividend stability is not an incidental by-product of a well-run company. The company's *willingness* (cultural) and *ability* (economic) to pay the dividend should be the beginning of our

**FIGURE 9-3**

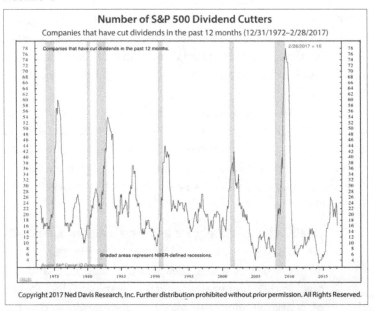

### Number of S&P 500 Dividend Cutters
Companies that have cut dividends in the past 12 months (12/31/1972–2/28/2017)

analysis and process. Figure 9–3 shows an unsurprising correlation between companies that cut their dividend and recessionary conditions.

The "tell" of this chart is that a lot of companies are highly exposed to cyclical economic conditions. There is certainly nothing surprising about that—if a good portion of companies were not negatively impacted by a recession, it probably wouldn't be a recession! But it is my conviction that a dividend can be stable and sustainable, even when economic conditions worsen. And a significant part of being able to continue paying the dividend is to not pay one recklessly to begin with! Let's unpack what responsible dividend payments look like, what financial metrics can tell us, and what we mean by "willingness" and "culture."

The "dividend payout ratio" is the percentage of net income paid out as dividends. Too low of a dividend payout ratio, and you might have a company hesitating to properly compensate their shareholders. Too high of a dividend payout ratio, and you might have a company susceptible to a dividend cut during tough times. The payout ratio is a crucial decision that requires finesse, prudence, shareholder alignment, and wisdom in the corporate finance suite.

Chapter 10 is going to make the distinction between "high yield" and "growth of yield," but that failure to delineate is at the core of where a lot of the subject of dividend sustainability can go wrong. Allow me to ask another question—do you see the difference, in judging dividend sustainability only, between these two stocks?

- ▶ One has a $50 share price and pays a $2 dividend (a 4% yield). Last year it also paid $2, but had a $80 stock price. So the stock is much cheaper than last year, and the yield is 60% higher than it was a year ago. The income, of course, is identical. Many managers didn't like the stock at a 2.5% yield, but now with a 4% yield are very intrigued.

- ▶ The other stock is also $50 and pays a $1.87 annual dividend (a 3.75% yield). Last year it paid $1.70; and the year before that paid $1.50. It has grown the dividend 10-15% per year for six years in a row. The stock price has also grown 10% or so per year (though for one year in that period, it was more or less flat on the year).

Which stock would be a more compelling buy to many so-called "value" managers? The first one has so much of what value methodology likes: a cheap (or cheaper) price, a high yield, a low P/E (price-earnings ratio), and so forth. But what does the dividend growth objective care about more between these two? Fundamentally, without knowing other key information, we see one company that "grew up to its yield," and another company "shrunk down to its yield." The intentionality matters! Not all yields are created equal. Getting excited about a yield going up because a stock price is dropping is like getting excited to lose weight by having the flu—*trust me, it is not the way you want it to happen, and the outcome is not sustainable.*

There is no reason to necessarily believe a company with a superficially interesting yield is inherently poised for dividend growth; in fact, empirical data would tell us that "accidental high-yielders" are extremely vulnerable for a dividend cut. The key challenge is to do the two things that are hardest to do for retail investors, and even for many professional money managers, but that actually represent the real "secret sauce" of this chapter: *One must be able to ignore stock price, and even ignore "yields," and just focus on the actual income statement and actual balance sheet of the company.*

Stock prices do not tell us about cash flow, or about cash flow coverage. Stock prices often do not even tell us about organic earnings, let alone earnings growth. All "yields" involve the stock price, because it serves as the denominator in the calculation. If one wants to look at the fundamental metrics of a business that speak to dividend sustainability, they can look beyond the stock price—but really, they *must* look beyond the stock price. The variety of metrics we are now going to discuss that do matter are all going to have one significant factor in common: You do not need the stock price involved.

The stock price is heavily influenced by sentiment on any given day. It is heavily affected by macro conditions. Interest rates in the economy impact P/E ratios. Headline events and "noise" impact daily pricing. For our purposes here, we are trying to determine the sustainability of a dividend, and the likelihood it will be increased in the future. Ours is an evaluation of the strength of the company's defense (balance sheet, ability to withstand difficulty, and other factors), *and* its offense (growth strategy, free cash flow, market share, and so on). No part of the future dividend payment is revealed in the stock price. Transcending noise is a very good idea for almost all serious students of the stock market, but it is particularly important in this fundamental exercise regarding the dividend's health.

The ability to pay the dividend can be initially analyzed using the following economic metrics:

1. **Dividend payout ratio.** Is there "wiggle room" to maintain the dividend if earnings decline from present levels? Does the rolling average of earnings volatility suggest that the payout ratio could be maintained without forcing the company to borrow money or deplete balance sheet assets to continue paying the dividend? There is not a set formula for each and every company as to what is most prudent, because each industry, sector, and company exists with different cyclical realities, seasonal conditions, order flows, inventory management, capex (capital expenditure) needs, and other variables that dictate a prudent payout ratio.

   An aggressively high payout ratio at best warrants a look at run-rate earnings expectations (does a company paying out too high a percentage of current earnings in dividends have a likelihood of growing net income in the year ahead well past the present dividend payout level?). Worst case, it could suggest the possibility of a dividend cut. And the middle level indicator is that the dividend may not be cut any time soon, but is an unlikely candidate for growth any time soon. Dividend growth investors want growing earnings, but they want a dividend payout ratio of those earnings that provides room for more growth and defense against the cyclicities of that business.

2. **Free cash flow.** Out of the thousands of times I have obsessed over a company's financials in my career, I have spent substantially more time evaluating free cash flow than I have earnings. One could argue (and they would be right) that in the long run, cash flows and earnings should converge. But as I quoted Keynes earlier, "in the long run, we are all dead." The nature of accrual accounting, the impact of marks to asset values, various factors like depreciation and amortization, how companies record certain revenues, and so on, all lead to significant complexity in the way "earnings" are reported versus the way we study free cash flow.

   In the most basic of senses, cash flow tells us everything we want to know, and nothing we don't want to know. Earnings can be "gamed"—particularly as they pertain to the sustainability of a dividend payment. But "operating cash flow" just tells us how a company is doing in terms of the revenues it [actually] brings in, and the money it [actually] spends. The free cash flow's coverage of the dividend is the vital ingredient in judging the dividend health of a company.

3. **Earnings consistency.** Many phenomenal companies may be excluded from those earnestly screening for reliable dividend growth because many great companies have excessively high earnings volatility, and highly cyclical businesses are difficult to trust as faithful dividend growers. Dividend growth investing can often require a willingness to bypass certain exciting, cyclical businesses—instead focusing on more stable, reliable earnings streams. Consumer staples, utilities, and telecom tend to be less volatile in terms of their profit generation. Generally speaking, the "things we have to

own" (household products, electricity, housing, medicine, wireless, water, power, auto, and the like) make for less volatile earnings rides, and therefore more trust in the dividend.

4. **Balance sheet.** It seems incomprehensible to ever make a determination about a company's prospects without knowing its balance sheet, but it is particularly futile to try and understand the dividend safety without knowing the quality of the company's assets, the liquidity picture, and the embedded leverage that could represent the biggest threat to the company's dividend growth.

A company's balance sheet is comprised of its *assets*, which equal *liabilities* plus *shareholder equity*. The two sides of the equation are always balanced. Assets divided by liabilities is a pretty common measure, but knowing the short-term assets versus short-term liabilities is especially important to understand liquidity safety. The debt-to-assets ratio gives us an idea of how much risk leverage is on the balance sheet; when combined with percentage of income debt service, you may get a good picture of the relative strength of a given company. Interest expense is reflected on the income statement, not the balance sheet, but the level and composition of debt being serviced is reflected on the balance sheet. No dividend payment can be assessed without this information.

Without getting too granular here, the covenants behind particular debts and bank credit lines warrant understanding, as does the company's debt term structure. For example, we knew in 2009 that the Federal Reserve was putting tight restrictions on the dividends financial firms would be allowed to pay. But most banks have similar covenants and ratio requirements in their debt agreements about a company's dividend payments. This is worth understanding to have a comprehensive view of dividend growth likelihood.

Companies that have a significant amount of complexity on their balance sheet and income statement particularly warrant an understanding of real organic cash flows. It should be worth pointing out for the rest of time the way the financial firms fooled everyone in late 2007 and early 2008.

I use Citigroup as an example because it was one near and dear to my experience. Throughout 2007, the company was paying a $2.20 annual dividend on what was roughly a $50 stock price (the stock has since done a one-for-ten reverse stock split, so today's price must be divided by ten to be comparable to pre-split prices). That yield equated to something near 5%, and by the end of the year, with the stock price down into the $30s, it had reached a 6–7% annual level. And yet, while inexplicably maintaining the dividend at its last quarterly meeting of 2007, the company sold 5% of itself to Abu Dhabi just weeks later with an 11% coupon payment requirement! The opacity of the balance sheet and distortions of the income statement left investors with no real way to evaluate the dividend sustainability (besides common sense). *A good rule of thumb—if a company is borrowing money or selling equity at an 11% cost, the 5% dividend is probably in trouble!* Within a couple of months, the dividend would be cut 40%, and eventually 100%.

The quantifiable and economic metrics are pivotally important to know, study, and analyze, yet even they are not as important as the *cultural propensity—the willingness—to protect and grow the dividend.* This criterion requires judgment of management and likely represents the single most neglected of all stock analysis criteria.

A CEO who is a "deal junkie" may sometimes pull off a high-profile acquisition that has the media fawning over him or her. Corporate boards that seek deal after deal can be praised for their aggressive engagement with competition. And yet, I would suggest that in studying decades of M&A activity in corporate America, nothing has created a bigger threat to solid dividend payer culture and economics than ill-considered mergers and acquisitions.

This does not mean that all M&A is a bad idea. Many transactions offer strategic benefits and cost synergies that are highly accretive to dividend growth. Some of the great dividend payers in the market have created their dividend capacity through well-executed inorganic transactions. But too often, large deals add reckless debt to the balance sheet, require a greater cash flow coverage to service the debt than is responsible (given dividend levels), and end up resulting (through time) in a real threat to the dividend.

M&A dysfunction is not the only cultural malady we seek to screen out. We distinguish between companies who are earnestly looking to expand the dividend payment to shareholders versus those who do so, but are brought kicking and screaming to that point. Management must have a grasp in their external communications and internal philosophy of how to balance profits reinvested in the growth of the business with returning cash to shareholders. Too many C-suite operators are untruthful, reckless, poor communicators, and generally disinterested in the whole concept of returning cash to shareholders.

Perhaps the caveat that "past performance is no guarantee of future results" need not contradict this obvious fact: *Companies that have a rich history of dividend growth provide a good view into management culture.* I cannot guarantee that a company that has grown their dividend for twenty or thirty or forty or fifty straight years will continue to grow it; but I sure have strong evidence that they want to!

In conclusion, the fact that dividend cuts, especially when resulting in an aggregate decline in portfolio income year-over-year, would jeopardize this entire book's thesis, is not worth disputing—but the idea that such a thing cannot be avoided, is. An active, diligent, meticulous, coherent process around evaluating a firm's ability and willingness to maintain and grow their dividend starts with real life economic analysis, and includes qualitative, cultural, and intuitive reasoning. The results of such a process ought to be a highly defensive portfolio that avoids the perils of dividend cuts on an individual basis, and therefore across a whole portfolio.

And that results in a growing dividend stream that leads to an appreciating asset base, creating successful outcomes for investors in both the accumulation and withdrawal stages of life.

# 10

## CLEARING UP CONFUSIONS
### High Yield vs. Growing Dividends

*"If companies don't know they can run out of money, they won't be thinking of ways not to run out of money."*

—BILL GROSS

*"Don't worry about the income. Worry about the outcome."*

—WARREN BUFFETT

A "straw man" logical fallacy is when one misrepresents the position of one's opponent, defeats that misrepresented position in argument, and then asserts that one actually refuted the opposing position. It is usually done on purpose, and it is not only fallacious in a logically academic sense, but is unfair and unhelpful in a real-life, practical sense, as well. Most of the time, a "straw man" is constructed on purpose—to help deal with difficult arguments one doesn't want to deal with, or to cover up for a lack of preparation and confidence. But sometimes, I believe a "straw man" argument is made out of well-meaning ignorance. Thoroughly refuting a position your opponent holds is satisfying, but all the more so if your opponent actually holds it.

I have been listening to critics of dividend growth investing for years, yet I have heard very little actual criticism of dividend growth investing. Whether on purpose or out of sincere misunderstanding, critics of dividend growth methodology spend the majority of their time critiquing a position that dividend growth advocates do not hold to, and that I have spent significant effort in this book actually repudiating.

In a spirit of graciousness, I will assume that much of this has been of the genuine confusion variety. It's a straw man argument all the same, but often I am confident the intentions are not sinister. Much of this misunderstanding has to do with how advocates of dividend growth investing articulate their own message. The purpose of this chapter is to provide the right clarity around the key distinctions of the investment philosophy I am proposing in this book.

The "straw man" critique I refer to is often a derivative of confusing "high yield" equity investing with "dividend growth" investing. Put differently, the argument is framed around the percentage yield instead of the percentage of growth.

In fairness to the straw-man critics, I hear dividend equity advocates all the time praising the merits of "dividend stocks," and, indeed, perhaps now even in Chapter 10, you think I have written a book about "dividend stocks." But I haven't. I have written a book about "growth-of-dividend" stocks. It would be malpractice to not differentiate these two things while I still have your attention.

This is not mere semantics. The term "dividend stock" does not describe any of the things that I have argued are important in this book. Lacking additional context, it could very well be interpreted as a vanilla advocacy for any situation where a stock is paying a dividend. And if all that is required is the mere existence of a dividend, it stands to reason that a "big dividend" is better than a "less big dividend." In other words, "high yield" doesn't just refer to junk bonds anymore! When the dividend growth world is confused for high yield stocks, pedestrian conclusions that "the higher the yield, the better" will abound. It is a forgivable confusion, and can only be rectified by a constant clarity and precision in the formulation of the dividend growth school of thought.

My argument in this book is not for "high dividend" stocks; it is for "high growth of dividend" stocks. I want stocks that offer growth. I want stocks that offer income. But I want stocks that offer growth-of-income. *That* is the objective of this investment philosophy. And it must be contrasted against what I am very much *not* advocating for.

What I am not advocating for is the mere acquisition of a high current yield, with no regard for why that yield got so high—did the income go up, or did the stock price come down— and with no regard for the sustainability of the dividend or its outlook for growth!

Our methodology starts with companies that offer a current yield higher than that of the S&P 500. In theory, that means a stock with a 2% current yield could make its way into our portfolio (presently, the yield on the S&P 500 is 1.75%).

The next filter is what eliminates most companies from consideration. Generally speaking, we want to see dividend growth of 5% or more for the last five years. The *starting yield* is not the key variable.

Consider this first hypothetical scenario in Figure 10–1.[36]

A 4% yield at time of purchase, with an annual growth of the dividend of 4%. That income, after twenty years of reinvestment, turns into an impressive $86,000, equaling 17% of what was originally invested. Very few would shake their heads at this hypothetical scenario.

However, now consider this second hypothetical scenario, shown in Figure 10–2.

A 3% yield at time of purchase (so, 25% less than the prior hypothetical), with an annual growth of the dividend of 9.6% (a

**FIGURE 10–1**

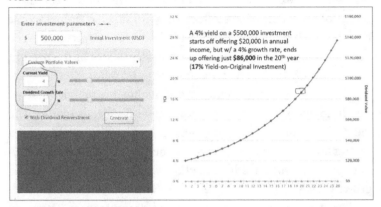

**FIGURE 10–2**

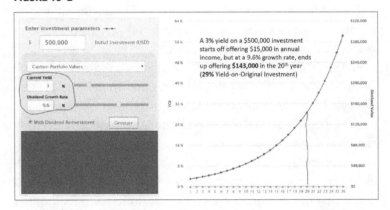

growth rate we are quite fond of; see Chapter 9). That income, after twenty years of reinvestment, turns into $143,000, 66% higher than the other example! This equals a 29% yield on what was originally invested. When framed this way, who would not take a 3% starting yield over a 4% one?

This is not to say we do not like "high yields." It is most certainly to say, though, that we have to like *why* the yield is high,

125

and what we expect to come from that in the future. There are plenty of situations where a stock sits with a high current income and the stock price is misunderstood or under-appreciated. The key ingredient, though, would never be the allure of the present yield, but rather our belief about its sustainability.

The quality of the company and its business model matter. The fundamentals driving the company's financials matter. The yield spread of the company versus its historical yield spread matters. And of course, prospects for the company's free cash flow growth matters (a lot). In other words, intelligent dividend growth investing does not rely merely on a high current yield. Rather, it depends on a whole milieu of circumstances. There are too many negative reasons a company could offer a high current yield, and those factors can only be avoided by having a thoughtful process around what one is buying, and why. If that process consists of nothing more than "buying high yield," it is not likely to end well. If, on the other hand, the process is rooted in a search for quality, sustainability, value, and opportunity, the present high yield a security offers could very well be very attractive.

My friends at Miller/Howard Investments put it the way shown in Figure 10–3.

As previously stated, some degree of current income is necessary to introduce us to the company. Stocks offering a yield below that of the market are eliminated from consideration, as are stocks with a questionable track record of dividend growth.

An interjection is warranted here: This does separate the approach described in this book from two very different "dividend strategies."

1. The traditional "aristocrats" often include some stocks who are faithful-as-can-be growers, but offer brutally low yields (as the market prices in their known dividend growth).

**FIGURE 10–3**

2. High yield stocks bought as members of the ninth or tenth decile of income level,[37] but that do not offer the growth-of-income we most cherish.

The first strategy often does not entice us enough with current income (the base from which great growth-of-income would go to work). The second strategy is highly vulnerable for all of the reasons we have already outlined.

The major "straw men" arguments against "dividend investing" do not apply to the subject of this book, because this book is about bottom-up investing in real companies with attractive fundamentals, quality management aligned with shareholders, and free cash flow that grows consistently. The right way to do dividend growth investing is not to buy companies whose dividend is starving the company from needed future growth, but rather those whose dividend indicates impressive future growth!

Is that easy to do? No, it is not. But the work that goes into this strategy is well worth it to avoid the pain and misery that thoughtless "high yield" investing can create. What can go wrong with just buying the highest yielders and letting nature run its course?

For starters, "high yield" can very often mean "no yield." Companies paying an unsustainable dividend (see Chapter 9) with deteriorating business conditions very easily become dividend cutters. If things worsen enough, they eliminate the dividend. It may not surprise you to learn that companies under pressure from their creditors are not encouraged to continue giving away cash to common stockholders!

Chapter 9 laid out this distinction further, but allow me to offer a refresher: too many high yield stocks became so by accident. Their stock prices dropped (presumably due to deteriorating business conditions) and the math of it all resulted in an "accidental high yielder."

Consider this: Company ABC's stock is at a $100 price and offers shareholders a $5 dividend, fresh off of a long period of earnings growth and solid business execution.

*$5 dividend divided by $100 = 5% yield*

But Company ABC starts to face challenges. They lose key clients. Their business model is being questioned by the market. Profits are declining. The stock price drops 50% (to $50/share), but the company board of directors has not yet reduced the dividend (knowing that to do so would make the stock price drop even further).

*$5 dividend divided by $50 = 10% yield*

So knowing those scenarios, does that 10% yield look attractive? Of course, it very well could be. Perhaps the market has overreacted to the company's challenges, and $75 would be a more reasonable stock price. Perhaps they have a reorganization plan that will protect the dividend but re-finance debt and re-strategize their business model. The point is, the 10% yield in this case came about as a negative occurrence and is in no way an automatic signal to snap it up.

Yet what do I hear constantly?

*"XYZ is paying 10%."*

*"My friend invested in a property and gets a risk free 12%."*

*"I like 4% yields, but can you get me something paying 7%?"*

The philosophical focus on dividend growth I advocate for in this book is not rooted in the immoral insinuation that reward can ever be divorced from risk. That is the unstated implication in blindly touting "high yields." Rather, our focus is to buy into the genius of free enterprise, where high quality businesses provide a product or service that is as non-cyclical and defensible as possible. That genius is well-embodied in the S&P 500, but we take it further for all of the reasons written about in prior chapters: we believe an attractive and sustainable dividend offers us higher quality companies, provides a buffer of downside protection in periods of market distress, and generates significant mechanical advantages for both the accumulator and the withdrawer. What we *do not* believe is that there is some free lunch to be had if someone just buys the highest yield they can find.

The security selection process we utilize has a lot of layers, but one of them is not—and never will be—a "reach" for high yield. Consider the following:

- ▶ Universe limited to companies offering current yield > S&P 500 yield.
- ▶ Further purged to companies with dividend growth history, generally a minimum of > 5% per annum for last five years.

- ▶ Sustainability analysis of the dividend around:
  - ▪ Payout ratio
  - ▪ Balance sheet
  - ▪ Cyclicality of earnings
- ▶ Free cash flow analysis
- ▶ Qualitative analysis:
  - ▪ Do we understand the business?
  - ▪ Do we like the business?
  - ▪ Does the business model lend itself to transparency and comprehensibility?
  - ▪ Management culture
  - ▪ Dividend inclinations
  - ▪ Governance
- ▶ Idiosyncratic factors:
  - ▪ What are catalysts to growth?
  - ▪ Is there an under-appreciated story?

You will note this is an entirely "bottom up" process—we are not looking to "hug" an index, or replicate the S&P 500, or match up to some requirement of sectors or market capitalizations. This approach to investing tends to find a lot more large cap companies (or good-sized mid cap companies) than any other options, just because of the focus on mature businesses that are ready to be consistent dividend payers and growers. But the philosophy of dividend growth is inherently "bottom up," a pursuit of companies that meet the investment criteria we have outlined herein.

I often hear the rather unimpressive argument that dividend stocks are "bond proxies"—that investing this way essentially just makes one interest rate sensitive in their portfolio, but with added equity market volatility. This is a different straw man argument—close cousins with the first—but it is even flawed in what it is disingenuously trying to criticize. First, the so-called "bond proxies" referred to—considered by these detractors generally to be the utilities, REIT, and telecom sectors—most certainly do function with a lower volatility level than the broad equity markets. But again, we are not looking with dividend growth investing to buy the bond proxies, mere fixed income surrogates. The entire point is to transcend "fixed" income!

And this tees up an extremely important point about the "bottom up" nature of proper dividend growth investing. It is not sector focused, but rather it is company focused!

Is it true that there are more dividend growers in the pharmaceutical industry than the consumer discretionary sector? Probably so. Is it true that "old tech" companies are more likely to pay stable dividends than "new tech" social media companies? Surely it is. But the point I am making is that the sector is incidental to the selection methodology, not a driver of it. And furthermore, it is a moving target. Many technology companies that are leading dividend payers today were zealously against dividend payments fifteen to twenty years ago (Cisco, Microsoft, Apple). We do not have to say, "we like consumer staples," or "we dislike materials." We like them all *if* they are capable dividend growers who meet our criteria! And we dislike them all if they don't. Some degree of sector diversification is generally a helpful risk mitigator, but it is not a driver of security selection for the focused dividend growth investor.

In conclusion, this book is about investing in companies that grow their profits, and from those profits grow the dividends they pay their shareholders. This book is not about companies with a "high yield"—it is not proposing a grab for "coupon"—and it is not about the mere accumulation of dividends. Our focus is on sustainable dividends, reflecting a high-quality company with a defensible business model.

High yield investing is for speculators, or amateurs.

Dividend growth investing is the essence of free enterprise.

# CONCLUSION

## Summarizing the Case for Dividend Growth Investing in a Post-Crisis World

*"A stock dividend is something tangible—it's not an earnings projection; it's something solid, in hand. A stock dividend is a true return on the investment. Everything else is hope and speculation."*

—RICHARD RUSSELL

I opened this book describing how the first ten years of this new millennium set the stage for so much of what drove my discovery process and led to the investment philosophy convictions I describe in this book. I will now conclude the book by discussing the last ten years.

I do not believe that the period of time covering the 1999 dotcom/tech crash through the financial crisis of 2008 changed principles of investing. I do believe investing in a post-crisis world ought to look different than it largely did pre-2008, or pre-1999. This is not because what I am proposing is right now, but was wrong then; it is because it was right then, too, but had been largely forgotten or misunderstood for too long.

Then and now, we live in a culture that obsesses with selection and timing, and that focus on selection and timing is either explicitly or implicitly accompanied by a lie: that one can successfully "time" the market—through proper charting, or studying, or the guidance of a guru, or reading of certain tea leaves, and so on—and thereby achieve the investment results one wants, devoid of the downside volatility one wishes to avoid.

People use modern technology to feed this cultural phenomenon—either through the information that feeds it or the instrumentation used in its execution. I am the last one to fear technological advancement or innovation; in fact, I see the continued progress in history as part of what we invest in every day when we invest in the profit-seeking capital of dividend growth stocks. But over the last twenty years we have seen online trading, Twitter, internet chat rooms, leveraged ETFs, and any number of other products, forums, mediums, and so forth—all by-products of a modern technologized era with various potentially positive uses—become enablers and tools in the dark side of this selection-and-timing-the-market myth.

Second only to the aforementioned folly of timing the market is the folly of chasing "hot strategies." Whether it be a hot fund, or hot manager, or hot "style," performance chasing—out of the rearview mirror—is all too common, and the way it ends is all too predictable. So often, what was working yesterday is exactly what will *not* be working tomorrow. We confuse luck with skill. And we confuse momentum with fundamentals.

More than anything else, this preoccupation with timing and selection reflects a cultural value system that is understandable, yet all too unfortunate: the easy buck, the painless gain, the quick buck, the easy way out.

There are various ways to approach investing that do not fall for the selection and timing traps. None of them, however, allow investors to escape facts that are, by definition, inescapable.

Quick and easy returns are evasive. Money that is to last a long time can take a long time to accumulate.

And to generate a sustainable cash flow that represents a premium return to the risk-free rate, one will be exposed to some kind of risk.

The risk I find most palatable—from a goal-achievement standpoint, even if not always from a human psychology standpoint—is market fluctuation risk. "Up and down" volatility is not always pleasant; but in a diversified portfolio, it does not blow someone up. ("Blowing up" may or may not be the scientific term, but it is the experience we in the business are tasked with avoiding at all costs).

Inflation risk with fixed income can become impossible to overcome.

Over-concentration risk can be fatal.

Excessive leverage carries a solvency risk when things turn against you that can also be devastating.

But market volatility will not kill you, and that which doesn't kill you makes you stronger. Portfolio resilience comes from quality, from diversification, and from the discipline and behavior of the one holding the portfolio.

Can market volatility have a mechanical impact on one's portfolio in their withdrawal phase, though? Yes, it can, and we looked at what "bad timing" risk can mean if one is withdrawing from a rapidly declining equity portfolio for sustained periods of time in Chapter 5. Adequate cash reserves can and should buffer much of this. But if market volatility is to be the great "risk" investors have to contend with once they have fled the maladies of a timing-and-selection culture, then I believe that "risk" can be made perfectly acceptable for the withdrawer through dividend growth investing.

Can market volatility rattle the cage of a growth-oriented accumulator of assets? Even apart from one still adding to their portfolio (such as a worker with a 401k plan, or an earner just periodically adding to their investment pool), a "lump sum" investor—someone who received an inheritance at age forty but doesn't want to touch it until age sixty, for example—may be particularly bothered by market fluctuation, even if they are not yet withdrawing from the portfolio. Adding new outside money to the portfolio at lower prices is not always possible, yet seeing new investments working in the portfolio via the reinvestment of dividends is always possible for the accumulator through dividend growth investing.

Post-crisis, financial markets have been rather robust, which is to be expected coming out of a severe market trough. The fundamentals of profits bottoming, then re-growing, make for solid equity returns. Add in a low rate environment pushing market multiples up and there has been little to complain about for risk asset investors. European markets have not enjoyed the same level of recovery (this has more to do with a European policy framework than anything else) and Japan has also sputtered in the midst of its final innings of a generational deflationary spiral. Commodities have been up and down, as have emerging markets. Credit has performed quite well (high yield bonds, bank credit), although credit is historically correlated high with equities. It has been a bull market for risk assets all around, and that has been most visible in the U.S. equity markets.

Bull markets do as much to distort smart thinking as bear markets do; the only thing worse than holding to an unwise behavior when it isn't working is holding to one when it is. The latter emboldens bad behavior, and creates less barriers to the consequences of unwise decisions.

I am well aware that it is difficult to stay focused on the wisdom of a 4% dividend yield that grows at 7.5% per year, when a hot tech stock may be going up 70% per year. If it is hot and flashy you are after, this book was not for you and a portfolio of dividend growth stocks will really not be for you.

But maybe, just maybe, hot and flashy is not all it is cracked up to be. The dotcoms of 1999 turned into the meltdowns of 2000. Lest we forget, it was not just Pets.com that became casualties of the technology bubble; companies no less important than

Cisco and Microsoft spent most or all of the last two decades underwater from their bubble-level stock prices. The Florida condo-flipping of 2006 turned into the epicenter of a financial crisis that brought the country to its economic knees. If one is looking for goals-based investing solutions that steer clear of 1999 dotcoms and 2006 condo-flipping, dividend growth is the strategy I feel best marries appreciation to income, accumulation to preservation, and value to growth.

The 1990s caused too many investors to capitulate to greed, euphoria, and lofty expectations unrooted to reality. I do not merely mean that investors came to believe in returns which were far too high, historically, and were far too easy to achieve. I mean that investors failed to understand what generates returns on capital in financial markets. The notion that profits didn't matter, that investors had infinite levels of patience for financial stability to be found, that haphazard business models could succeed in globally competitive marketplaces—these notions had to be painfully corrected. Throughout the go-go 1990s, dividend growth investing performed just fine—if "just fine" means "achieving the returns you need to succeed in your financial goals."

The 2000–2009 period saw a huge crash, a huge rally, and another huge crash. The defensive characteristics of dividend growth investing would have served investors relatively quite well in that period, but the offensive elements of positive cash flow (for withdrawers) and reinvesting at lower prices (for accumulators) would have been even more impactful.

The last decade has seen dividend growth excel in certain years, and lag in others, but like all risk assets, perform well. The environment in which we find ourselves as of press time, though, has become one where, once again, fundamentals seem boring. Double-digit returns seem easy and hot-dot chasing seems reasonable. No part of the last three decades has served to improve embedded deficiencies in human nature itself.

Fundamentals, foundational principles, and disciplined behaviors mattered before the financial crisis, too, but I would like to think there was a super-charged lesson in their importance imprinted in our psyches by the crisis. Dividend growth investing is meant to be the full embodiment of fundamental, disciplined, foundational, behavioral investing. It does not pretend market volatility is avoidable, yet it does seek to harness this to its advantage. It recognizes the basic business reality of where free cash flow and profits come from, and how dividends from such can be sustained and grown. It puts the focus on company performance, and not the madness of the crowds. It does not pretend to be able to "game the system" or to time the market or to outsmart The Man. It is a system in which the risks are known: there will be market price volatility; you will miss out on certain hot dot stocks. It strikes right at the heart of all investment objectives—the return of cash to the investor.

We have had plenty of excuses to vary from fundamentals and foundational principles in the last twenty to thirty years— euphoric bubbles, panic collapses, and the like. Yet through it all, the dividend growth orientation would have provided growth at a seemingly miraculous level for those accumulating future income, and for those protecting current income against both absolute decline and inflationary decline.

There will never be a time that dividend growth investing is advocated for "tactical" or "timely" reasons by this author. In periods of low interest rates, high interest rates, low inflation, high inflation, weak stock markets, strong stock markets, risk on, risk off, I believe dividend growth investing to be the wisest way to gain exposure to equity returns.

Yes, the tax law changes of 2003 and 2013 helped reinforce the case. And yes, the long-term, secular period of underwhelming interest rate alternatives in the cash and bond markets make dividend equity investing more compelling. But the fundamental arguments as laid out in Chapters 3, 4, and 5 rely on no such tactical tailwind. The mechanical and mathematical realities of compounding reinvested dividends apply in any market environment. The growing stream of always rising cash flow suits the needs of withdrawers in any season. Some degree of inflation always needs to be overcome. And if anything from this book needs to be restated in this conclusion, it is this: *the embedded company quality lift in the world of dividend growth lends itself to a superior portfolio for those who care about risk management, balance sheet strength, and management alignment with shareholders.*

I stated earlier that there are various ways to approach investing that transcend the cultural propensity for timing and selection. Various disciplines and systems of investing share at least this much in common: *they do not claim to deliver that which does not exist.* I wrote this book because I believe dividend growth to be the best of these systems in terms of simplicity, tax efficiency, risk-adjusted results, and mechanical optimization. I am not interested in claiming that in a certain window of time the dividend growth raindrop will fall down a window faster than another investment raindrop will. I am interested in defending, though, the idea that *some* methodology, consistently applied and administered with behavioral wisdom and discipline, will provide a better long-term result than the alternatives.

Let me put that differently. In our firm, we wish to pull investors from the cult of selection and timing, and into the world of dividend growth equity with heavy behavioral modification overlaying all we do. As long as we are guiding decisions on behalf of our client's capital, dividend growth equity will be a major part of our investing strategy. The epiphany I had so many years ago sticks with me to this day—investors put capital to work because they want it back in the form of cash. They may want a stream of cash, or a higher lump sum of cash, and the timelines of re-delivery will vary just like the time the money is to be deployed will vary. But a return of cash is the be-all and end-all, and therefore we have a fiduciary responsibility to do this in the most efficient way possible.

For our money, that way is with the great companies of the world—liquid, well-managed, tax-efficient, with pricing power, aligned with shareholders, generating strong free cash flow, paying out a growing dividend to their investors. The underlying price of the stock of these companies will vary and fluctuate, of course, but that growing income will prove to be the return of cash the investor wants and needs, whether now or in the future.

This methodology has paid dividends to us and our clients for many years, and will do so for many years to come.

Investors like to say, "I want to own something that is real," often in reference to real estate or gold.

I can think of nothing more "real" than the dividend that comes from ownership in free enterprise. The miracle of free enterprise combined with the miracle of compounding returns forms a potent combination in this post-crisis investment environment. We like to call it: the miracle of dividend growth.

# APPENDIX I

## Dividend Growth in International Markets

*"When you consider the sheer magnitude of investable equities to choose from in the world's emerging markets, you realize that finding one that looks attractive enough to warrant investing your faith and assets in is as formidable a task as finding a needle in a haystack. Fortunately, researching investment opportunities is a lot more interesting than digging for needles in haystacks."*

—MARK MOBIUS

There were a lot of investor mistakes I sought to address in this book, not the least of which were avoiding the risk of negative compounding, properly distinguishing between speculation and investing, and not failing to appreciate the mechanics of your investments both as an accumulator and a withdrawer. To know the world of investing is to know the world of behavioral finance, for inevitably the financial mistakes one makes behaviorally are the predominant determinant of one's investing success or failure.

This appendix to the book seeks to address a potential behavioral mistake that too many investors make today, and seeks to tie that mistake to a distinct point of view about dividend growth investing in international markets.

The mistake I refer to is commonly called "home bias," and it is no more complicated than the tendency so many investors have to focus all their portfolio exposure in domestic equities—because they are familiar, knowable, and convenient—thereby missing out on the diversification and total return possibilities of a globally diversified portfolio.

Ironically, it is probably most forgivable when U.S. investors make this mistake. At least 43% of sales for S&P 500 companies come from overseas[38] so significant international exposure is embedded in U.S. equity markets. And U.S. capital markets are themselves the most sophisticated, innovative, and lucrative in the world. The dollar is the world's reserve currency. Our country has a well-respected rule of law. If one had to pick a single country to concentrate their portfolio in, they could do worse than the United States of America.

But we know the home bias condition is a defect in human nature, as the investors of countries who make up a miniscule fraction of global GDP suffer from the same epidemic. For example, an investor in Sweden may have 100% of their equity portfolio in Swedish (domestic) stocks, yet Sweden represents a tad less than 1% of world equity capitalization. This is not a by-product of the relative strength of the Swedish equity markets; it is merely human nature playing itself out. People invest in their own backyards. It is comfortable, it feels safe, and it addresses the human need for familiarity.

And yet, it takes away a diversifying benefit that investing across different geographic regions can have. From exposure to faster-growing markets, to potential diversification should U.S. markets struggle, international investing has been long known to offer a lowered systematic risk, with a diverse opportunity set attractive to many investors.

I have spent a whole book championing the cause of dividend growth investing, however, and no amount of "global growth" exposure or U.S. diversification justifies the abandonment of the dividend growth arguments I have made. My thesis herein, though, is that dividend growth is not only available in many international markets, providing the opportunity to diversify globally and achieve the risk/reward aspirations international investing is supposed to provide, but furthermore, that dividend growth itself is especially opportune in many international markets right now.

I spent the lion's share of my investing career ignoring Japanese equity markets, finding the macroeconomic environment (correctly) to be highly precarious, and believing that their corporate sector was in no position to assert a dividend growth culture I would be able to trust. In 2016, I began to believe that the worst of the macroeconomic conditions were behind them. (See Figure A–1.)

But further study also pointed to a tremendous opportunity (not assurance, but opportunity) for dividend growth within

**FIGURE A–1**

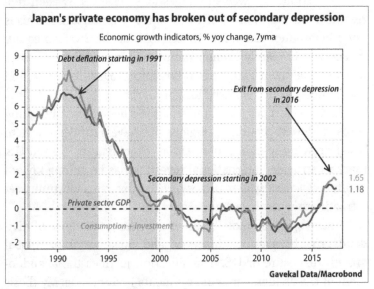

Japan's private economy has broken out of secondary depression

Economic growth indicators, % yoy change, 7yma

Gavekal Data/Macrobond

**FIGURE A–2**

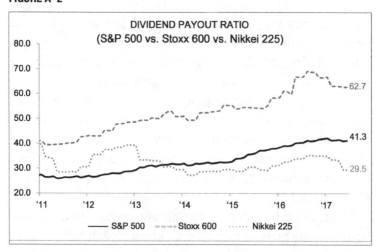

DIVIDEND PAYOUT RATIO
(S&P 500 vs. Stoxx 600 vs. Nikkei 225)

Japanese equity markets. (See Figure A–2.) For one thing, I noticed that Japan was way behind the rest of the world in the percentage of profits its companies were paying out as dividends.[39]

The opportunity set seemed quite compelling to me: A country coming out of a generational deflationary spell, with a massive need for investment income for its aging population, at a brutally low payout ratio now of its current profits, and with five trillion yen presently on the balance sheets of its public companies (meaning, the substantial ability to self-fund capital expenditures for the foreseeable future, thereby reducing the need to divert potential dividend payments to such expenses).

One cannot invest in Japan without risk. Their central bank has been interventionist in a way that makes Greenspan/Bernanke/Yellen look like Ayn Rand. Their demographics are challenged, in that they lack the youth and workforce to meet the productivity needs of the broad society. They are heavily indebted, and lack the organic GDP growth to address it the way other dynamic countries might.

But all of those are top-down concerns, and do not negate what may be a very attractive investment proposition in Japan over the next decade: A corporate sector that has bottomed, and is in need of organic dividend growth, with the Return on Equity, balance sheets, and profits growth to generate it.

Japan's profits are now growing at 6.5% per year, and dividends have grown at 9.5% per year for several years. Even with these growth rates, the present yield for a Japanese equity index investor still sits just around the 2.5% level, higher than the S&P 500, despite dramatically different conditions warranting more dividend yield.

It strikes this author as an entirely reasonable thesis that Japan's equity markets may offer dividend growth opportunities that help marry the dividend growth philosophy of this book to the diversification and return benefits of global investing.

But if the dividend growth potential in Japan is interesting, the opportunity for dividend growth in emerging markets is downright fascinating. Interestingly, that is not because the broad index of emerging market companies represents a great dividend play, but rather what we see as obtainable where active management focuses on dividend growth. (See Figure A–3.)

Even apart from absolute yields, let alone the rate of growth in dividends, the mere addition of dividend paying companies to the universe of emerging market stocks is something to behold. In the course of my professional investing career, that universe has doubled in size, a reflection of the maturation of emerging capital markets and growth in shareholder alignment and governance the space has experienced.

And yet, after twenty years of remarkable dividend growth, the payout ratio of emerging markets stocks remains lower than the United States, and much lower than Europe (though higher than Japan). (See Figure A–4.)

**FIGURE A–3**

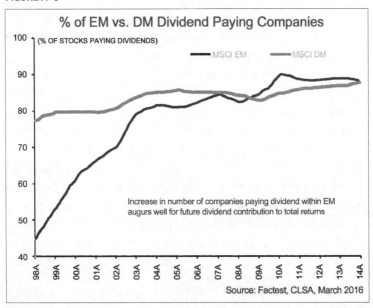

**FIGURE A–4**

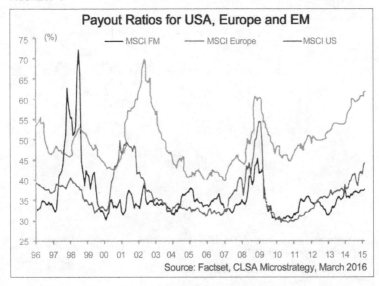

At a 35% current dividend payout ratio, but earnings growth of over 7% per year, and annual dividend growth that matches the earnings growth, one could easily see the dividend flows exponentially grow in the years to come.

The fact of the matter is that emerging markets offer a rare mix of growth and compelling value. Earnings growth is substantially higher than most developed markets, and valuations substantially lower. There is a reason for this: emerging markets investing contains currency risk, geopolitical risk, sometimes various degrees of liquidity risk, and are the textbook definition of violating our "home bias." (See Figures A–5, A–6, and A–7.) And yet, the metrics suggest, a compelling value for the investor who has properly digested the risks to the thesis.

Here, the thesis is not as easy as in U.S. markets. Companies do not have the dividend history that they often do in the States,

**FIGURE A–5**

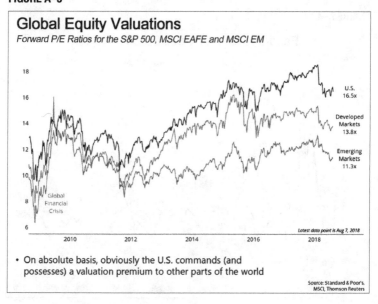

- On absolute basis, obviously the U.S. commands (and possesses) a valuation premium to other parts of the world

Source: Standard & Poor's, MSCI, Thomson Reuters

**FIGURE A–6**

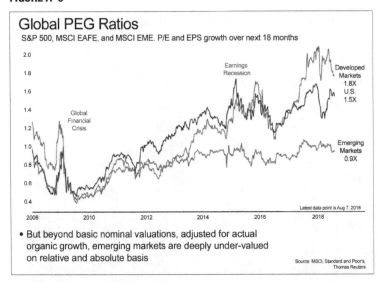

## Global PEG Ratios
S&P 500, MSCI EAFE, and MSCI EME. P/E and EPS growth over next 18 months

- But beyond basic nominal valuations, adjusted for actual organic growth, emerging markets are deeply under-valued on relative and absolute basis

Source: MSCI, Standard and Poor's, Thomas Reuters

**FIGURE A–7**

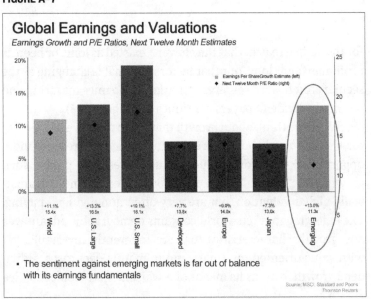

## Global Earnings and Valuations
*Earnings Growth and P/E Ratios, Next Twelve Month Estimates*

- The sentiment against emerging markets is far out of balance with its earnings fundamentals

Source: MSCI, Standard and Poor's Thomson Reuters

**FIGURE A–8**

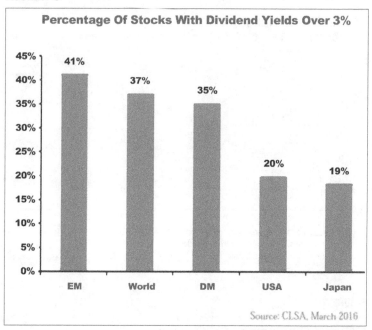

Percentage Of Stocks With Dividend Yields Over 3%

Source: CLSA, March 2016

for the simple reason that they haven't existed as long, or been as profitable for as long, or other factors. But that is changing as the secular shift towards emerging market companies maturing and becoming dividend payers continues (see Figure A–8).

When we think about growth that we do not have to over-pay for, we cannot help but think emerging markets represent a more opportunistic way for a value-oriented investor to pursue such growth. U.S. "growth" companies not only command a dramatically higher valuation, but are very often non-dividend-paying. The emerging markets world contains demographic advantages and growth characteristics that are inherently investable, yet with value-oriented multiples, and in many select cases, a dividend growth focus as its means of rewarding shareholders.[40] (See Figure A–9.)

**FIGURE A–9**

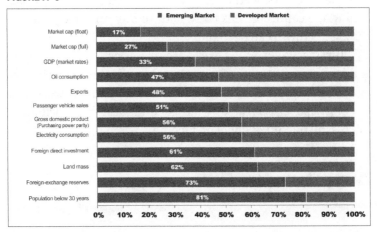

This investment thesis is not helpful without more specifics. I do not advocate buying the entire index of emerging markets stocks, where many companies pay no dividend at all, and where the index construction methodology lends itself to very large market capitalization companies primarily centered around their exporting to U.S. markets. The emerging markets space in general, and the dividend growth focus within emerging markets, will be best served through an active management approach where these fundamentals and philosophical objectives are valued.

Whether it be in Japan or emerging markets, there is risk in international investing. As in a U.S. equity portfolio, there will be market volatility; in fact, there could be more in international markets than U.S. markets. The opportunity set described in this appendix is rooted in the belief that home bias denies investors of a certain diversification and growth catalyst, and that secular and fundamental forces are lining up in Japan and the emerging markets space in particular in such a way as to offer dividend growth opportunity for equity investors.

Global diversification makes for a more holistic portfolio, and in the context of this book, adds to the "universe" whereby dividend growth can be found.

Investors all over the world are searching for cash to use in either the present or the future, in either a lump sum or in periodic withdrawals. Fortunately, investors all over the world can find *investments from all over the world* that can help facilitate a successful pursuit of dividend income.

# APPENDIX II

## Dividend Growth in the Context of a Fiduciary Standard

*"Sustainability is an important factor in the long-term success of a business. Therefore as with any other issue related to the prudent management of capital, considering sustainability is not only important to upholding fiduciary duty, it is obligatory. As the context of business and investing continues to shift, implementing a framework for allocating capital that embeds sustainability into it will be critical to successfully navigate the transition."*

—DAVID BLOOD, GENERATION INVESTMENT MANAGEMENT

"Fiduciary standard" is not exactly a household term, though it has picked up a lot of steam in the last several years. One of the reasons for the lack of familiarity with the term, even amongst the investing public, is the default presumption that many investors understandably have that "my advisor is required to act in my best interests," a presumption that not only is frequently false, but which also carries with it the presupposition that one's advisor is, well, an advisor.

Few issues in financial services have generated as much political heat as this so-called fiduciary controversy. At its core, the issue centers around the "obligation of duty" that someone engaged in financial services has. Those who are registered as "advisors" (regulated by the 1940 Investment Advisors Act) are bound by the fiduciary standard that mandates the highest standard of care to the client receiving the advice. It specifies that one's duty is to the client, and carries with it the attendant responsibilities that go with such a standard (transparency, disclosures, minimization if not elimination of conflicts of interest, and the like).

But more fundamentally, it speaks to the underlying governor of the relationship: that the advisor act in the client's *best* interests at all times—that the advisor place the client's needs above their own needs. The concept of fiduciary care carries significant legal implications, and is indeed an important word in the context of legality, regulatory responsibility, and technical meaning. However, it also can be said to be a highly *ethical* term, carrying a great deal of *moral* meaning and attendant obligations.

A fiduciary owes those under their care *uberrima fides*: utmost faithfulness. The language is all-encompassing, dramatic, superlative, and binding because the expectation one under fiduciary care has is all those things.

If the 1940 Investment Advisers Act defines the obligation of duty, and if common sense suggests that financial advisors should function as fiduciaries for their clients, then what is the controversy all about? Essentially, the vast, vast majority of those who hold themselves out as "advisors" are under no fiduciary standard at all. Better still, many go back and forth from a fiduciary standard to a much lower standard of care at will, changing hats the way a performer in a Broadway play does.

This is not a criticism of the people engaged in the brokerage profession; it is a commentary on an entire industry that lacks the precision in its nomenclature to effectively inform a consumer in it who does what. It is somewhat surreal, but it is a big deal, and it has direct relevance to the subject of this book.

A securities representative license will allow someone to hold themselves out as a "financial advisor," and indeed, they may very well be a really good one! But they are not under a legal requirement to act in their client's best interests. And their firm most certainly is not. They are obligated to make "suitable recommendations" and, I confess, suitable recommendations sound better than unsuitable ones. But no, most people do not wish to entrust their financial guidance and wellness to someone with a soft legal requirement and standard of care.

The vertical revenue model of the large Wall Street brokerage firms is not compatible with a fiduciary standard or a conflict-minimizing model. Receiving fees from money managers to be on your menu sounds like a good business decision for the firm, but not necessarily an alignment of interests between firm and client. From trading desks to distribution agreements with money managers, to manufacturing of their own product, to a barrage of lending products, to underwriting fees on new issues, to internal fees on proprietary product, the revenue model of today's financial services industry is, shall we say, ripe with conflicts of interest. And who administers the advice out of this somewhat problematic model? An employee of the firm, who owes his or her firm a high standard of loyalty, whose paycheck is signed by the firm he or she works for, to generate revenue by the sale of products.

You get the idea.

So am I "talking my book" here? As a recovered portfolio manager and wealth advisor at the Managing Director level of one of these big brokerage firms, who is now a fiduciary and independent advisor, do I not have a conflict or vested interest of my own here?

I sure do. I confess with full transparency: I really am obligated to operate as a fiduciary on behalf of my clients. At my business, all of our advisors owe full transparency about compensation and material information to our clients. We must be faithful to what is best for our clients each and every day. Our highest loyalty is to our clients, not a firm who employs us. We cannot be paid to sell product on behalf of a third party; we are compensated by our clients for the advice and service we give them. Guilty as charged. I am advocating for the fiduciary standard, and I happen to be under it myself. But far from being a conflict, this is the very definition of alignment.

What I or those who work with me speak about must be what we genuinely believe to be in the best interests of our clients, or we cannot and must not recommend it. A "set it and forget it" model of expensive mutual funds may be "suitable" for a given investor, but the construction, implementation, and monitoring of a portfolio like that is highly unlikely to be in the "best interest" of anyone. A constant rotation of the firm's "new product recommendations" is not in anyone's best interest, even if it checks the "suitability" box. Loading up a portfolio with hidden commission products that are not monitored after the point of sale does not drive the best outcome for an investor. Investors who are being properly served receive a coherent methodology, a defensible strategy, and an intelligent pursuit of risk/reward optimization. A financial plan as a veneer to sell a financial product (one that, shockingly, pays Mr. "Advisor" a substantial, and hidden, commission) is not a fiduciary plan. It is a scheme. It is a gimmick.

And it is a sad indictment of what too often passes for financial services in this day and age.

The world of dividend growth is not, and cannot be, a "product." It is not a sale. It is not a transaction. It is, at its core, a system of thought. It is a philosophy. It is a worldview. It is a process. It requires thoughtfulness, but it also requires application. It is a way to approach a portfolio, but it follows the plan that generates the profile for the portfolio. Absent intelligent, comprehensive planning, dividend growth is incoherent. It must be understood in the context of cash flow needs, tax ramifications, supplemental asset classes, liquidity, reserves, risk aversion, charitable intentions, employer stock, retirement plan options, real estate, timelines, inheritance expectations, elder care needs, child care needs, risk management, contingency planning, and everything else in your financial life.

Dividend growth is a way of thinking about the tools that will facilitate the successful achievement of one's financial goals. It cannot be used without a plan, or it will fail.

An inadequate plan, usually at the hands of one who is not functioning like a real fiduciary with *utmost faithfulness* to their client's needs, is why so many financial goals fail. The holistic and comprehensive landscape I just described requires the attention of someone with proper alignment, proper incentive, and the moral duty to care for the result.

There are any number of reasons a diligent, responsible, and fiduciary-minded advisor may disagree with the central tenets of this book from an investment philosophy standpoint. And I would rather that person manage your capital than someone who actually agrees with this book's tenets, but views it as a fund to sell and not as a holistic process. I mean that from the bottom of my heart. In the totem pole of risks that threaten one's financial wellness, the thoroughness of the advisor guiding your affairs is far more important than the particulars of the investment philosophy.

I certainly do believe that dividend growth is a thoughtful and investor-friendly way to build and protect financial capital. But for all my advocacy of dividend growth as a methodology, a mentality, and a movement, I would trade it all away for a fiduciary standard in financial services. Of course, there is no binary decision to make there, so it is an unnecessarily dramatic thing for me to say. One can have both, and that is what I deem best. That is what I have built my business around: *a fiduciary requirement that seeks to manage the accumulation, distribution, and preservation stages of our clients' financial lives.*

And when you put it that way, you can see why we get so fired up to talk about dividend growth.

*Uberrima Fides. Utmost Faithfulness,* indeed.

# ACKNOWLEDGMENTS

This book, my last book (*Crisis of Responsibility*), my entire career, and pretty much everything else I have striven to do in my adult life, was made possible by the love and support of my wife and best friend, Joleen. She is the blessing of my life, and her support of my life's calling is the best asset my calling has ever had.

Joleen and I have received three particular dividends of our own in Mitchell, Sadie, and Graham. My prayer for their life is that they appreciate the miracle of compounding, that they invest for what is real and not that which is speculative, and more than anything else, that they receive the dividends of truth, beauty, and goodness in the way they grow up to understand life and the world around them.

There are other professional acknowledgments I will make, but this book, on this topic, could never have happened if I had not been brought to the light of dividend growth investing by Miller/Howard Investments. Lowell Miller, their founder and Chief Investment Officer, mentored my appreciation for dividend growth investing in profound ways, and created a philosophical foundation in me that has served our clients for more than a decade, and will serve them for decades to come. Luke Theeuwes, you are a true professional. Woodstock, NY—who would have thought this conservative would have a reason to appreciate you so much?

There is a wealth management firm in Newport Beach, CA and New York City called The Bahnsen Group, where dividend growth investing is very much put to practice. The business has my name on the door, but it has the daily contributions of our team to thank for what it has become. Brian Szytel, Kimberlee Davis, Don Saulic, Robert Graham, Trevor Cummings, Sean Latimer, Deiya Pernas, Kenny Molina, Brian Tong, Glen Hall, Jackie O'Hare, Camille Mesite, Alexis Olgard, Ericca Murillo, Rayna Austin, Kelsey Thompson, and Brendan Sullivan—true professionals, fiduciaries, and friends.

If I name every client I am thankful for I will double the page count, but our clients deserve the dividends they have coming to them, and then some. Their faith and confidence is the core of our business. Because they trust us, we will never be anything but trustworthy.

Special thanks to (in no particular order): Mark and Carolynne Corigliano, Merv and Sharon Simchowitz, Andrea Shelly, Tracy Price, Stuart and Naomi Nagasawa, Ed and Lori Block, Patricia Spado, Kathy Bronstein, Julianna Pyott, Jocelyn Simon, Pete and Wendy Grande, Lloyd & Dana Taylor, Ed and Angela Grasso, Matt and Kat Smith, John and Alecia Kruger, Jan Moorad, Peter and Karen Burke, Rick and Denese Wahler, Cathy Holmes, Marion Smith, Mark Johnson, Andy and Leslie Cies, Jim and Donna Morrison, Mike Campbell, Gary and Roberta Luque, Keith and Pam Curry, Andrea Tennant, Tom and Laura Roche, Tim and Steph Busch, Joe Corigliano, Tom Grant, Bob Loewen, Larry and Nancy Silverberg, Tony DiGiovanni, Bob and Bobi Roper, Chris and Lottie Moody, Charlotte Evans, Tom and Lucy Butler, Steve Foigelman, Claude Centner, Rob Tholl and Adrienne Francis, Joe and Terri Gilman, Dennis and Patty Ambrose, Carollyn Hawkes, Michael and Adrienne Wienir, Carl and Bonnie Friedrich, and so, so, so many more.

Special thanks to Nick Murray, whose newsletters, mentorship, speaking, and writing over the years have created a ROI of infinity in my career.

Special thanks to Larry Kudlow, the walking embodiment of dividend-paying redemption, and who is my hero and friend.

I am thankful for my time at UBS and Morgan Stanley, for the friendships made, lessons learned, and experiences enjoyed.

Thank you to Rob Forrester, Kelly Friis, Chris Collie, Michael Gohlke, Rob Biddinger, Liz Cassel, Catherine Howse, Rob Cannon, and John Donovan, for your partnership, friendship, and support.

I am thankful to the HighTower organization for their legacy in driving a fiduciary standard and bringing first-class advisors from the dark side to the good side.

Thank you to Andy Johnson, Annie Scranton, Meghan Powers, Fred Whitaker, Michael Klarin, Steve Card, Mina Whitmer, Peter Van Voorhis, and so many more who have served The Bahnsen Group in various ways over the years, and who we are deeply appreciative for.

I thank God for King's College, who shall receive any and all royalties this book happens to provide, for being a light in the culture, and for bringing a dividend-paying institution to downtown New York City. The greatest city in the world needs a place like King's College. We have a lot of work to do, and that work will pay dividends.

National Review and Pacifica Christian High School remain my other two extra-curricular passions. One stands athwart history yelling stop, and the other teaches kids to think and live well. That is a division of labor I can invest in.

Thank you to Pastor Jon Tyson of Church of the City, NYC, who speaks the truth in love, and has embraced the concept of moral courage and intellectual adventure.

My agent, D.J. Snell, remains a friend and advocate, and I am so grateful for the work he has done on my behalf.

Once again, I am so grateful for my publisher, Post Hill Press, and particularly their CEO, Anthony Ziccardi. Anthony is a rare breed in the publishing world—deeply relational, totally communicative, extremely "bought in," and a true professional.

Thank you to those friends with whom I enjoy a sustainable, growing friendship. Aaron Bradford, Eric Balmer, Luis Garcia, Thomas Bonds, Gary Sully, Jim Nelson, Paul Murphy, Andrew Sandlin, Brian Mattson, Jeff Ventrella, Scott Albrecht, Brian Harrington, Jack Fowler, and too many more to count.

Thank you to family—Jonathan and Julie Bahnsen, Annika and Leila, Matthew and Katie; Uncle Brad (crispy bits count as dividends) and Aunt Vicki Bahnsen; Colin and Monica Robertson, Tate, Auden, and Lucy; Mike Dogg; Todd and Joclene White, Alexis, Jack, (fight on), Olivia, and Ava.

Speaking of cousin Monica, thank you for being a supreme editor, and for making me laugh. You are in my life forever, and I love you.

I reiterate my gratitude to the man this book is dedicated to, Darin Dennee. It would be impossible to capture my gratitude for what Darin meant in my life for the years in which my love of the stock market took hold. It also would be impossible to calculate how much better off all "dotcom era" investors would be if they had been accumulating growing dividends instead of chasing PASA throughout that period. But the journey trumps the destination.

And I thank the God who lifts me up out of the pit, out of the miry clay. He turned a speculative arrogant growth stock into a large cap dividend payer, and He did it because He loves me.

# ENDNOTES

1 "S&P 500 Annual Total Return Historical Data," YCharts.com, http://ycharts.com/indicators/sandp_500_total_return_annual.

2 "DJIA, S&P500, NASDAQ Yearly Returns Comparison," 1Stock1.com, www.1stock1.com/1stock1_142.htm.

3 Style box investing refers to apportioning one's portfolio into different boxes based on market capitalization (small, medium, and large), as well as style (growth, value, and core). It is a simplistic way to talk about asset allocation, at least in a basic manifestation.

4 FTSE Russell Indices, 1995-1999, http://www.ftse.com/products/russell-index-values.

5 Aswath Damodaran, "Annual Returns of Stock, T.Bonds and T.Bills: 1928 – Current," NYU Stern Business School, pages.stern.nyu.edu/~adamodar/New_Home_Page/datafile/histretSP.html. Information on this website is sourced from the Federal Reserve, St. Louis.

6 "DJIA, S&P500, NASDAQ Yearly Returns Comparison," 1Stock1.com.

7 Bespoke's Sector Weightings Report, 2018.

8 Annual Sector Total Return, Goldman Sachs Global ECS Research.

9 "Databases, Tables and Calculators by Subject," U.S. Department of Labor, Bureau of Labor Statistics, https://data.bls.gov/timeseries/LNS12000000. Information calculated for February 2008 to February 2010.

10 "The Great Recession: Over But Not Gone?" Northwestern Institute for Policy Research, 2014, https://www.ipr.northwestern.edu/about/news/2014/IPR-research-Great-Recession-unemployment-foreclosures-safety-net-fertility-public-opinion.html.

11 And because I believe in diversification and risk management, I see the wisdom in a multitude of companies being involved in that investment.

12 "Miller/Howard YOI Calculator," Miller/Howard Investments, http://www.mhinvest.com/yoi.html.

13 These hypothetical illustrations are performed at the YOI Calculator (Yield-on-Original Investment) at www.mhinvest.com, the website of Miller/Howard Investments. They do not project an actual stock's actual returns; they merely conduct the math of given inputs we (or anyone else) enters. The example in this paragraph contains one set of inputs; another example would contain different ones. The calculator is reliable for the math of the inputs, and nothing else.

14 These companies are not listed as recommendations whatsoever, but mere illustrations and reinforcements of how this math and concept I am describing has worked in my actual lifetime.

15 "S&P 500 Index, 90 Year Historical Chart," Macrotrends, https://www.macrotrends.net/2324/sp-500-historical-chart-data.

16 Lawrence C. Strauss and Evie Liu, "How Dividends Power Returns," *Barron's*, Dow Jones & Company, August 15, 2018, https://www.barrons.com/articles/how-dividends-power-returns-1534367649.

17 Figure 2, "The Power of Dividends: Past, Present, and Future," Insights: Hartford Funds (September 2018), https://www.hartford-funds.com/insights/featured-perspectives/ThePowerofDividends2.html.

18 "U.S. Quality Dividend Fund Growth," WisdomTree, p. 2, 2017, https://www.wisdomtree.com/etfs/equity/dgrw.

19 Figure 1 (original data source: Morningstar, 1/18), "The Power of Dividends: Past, Present, and Future," *Insights*: Hartford Funds (September 2018), https://www.hartfordfunds.com/insights/featured-perspectives/ThePowerofDividends2.html.

20 H. David Sherman and S. David Young, "Where Financial Reporting Still Falls Short," *Harvard Business Review* (July-August 2016), https://hbr.org/2016/07/where-financial-reporting-still-falls-short.

21 Lowell Miller, *The Single Best Investment*, Independent Publishers Group (2006): 44, Figure 3-3.

22 Lowell G. Miller, "The Power of Compounded Growth and Reinvested Dividends," *AAII Journal*, American Association of Individual Investors (June 2015): 2, Figure 1.

23 Lowell Miller, *The Single Best Investment*, 31.

24 "S&P 500 Annual Total Return Historical Data," 2000–08, YCharts .com, http://ycharts.com/indicators/sandp_500_total_return _annual.

25 Daniel G. Goldstein, Eric J. Johnson and William F. Sharpe, "Choosing Outcomes Versus Choosing Products," *Journal of Consumer Research* 35, no. 3 (2008): 440-456.

26 FANG is a common acronym assigned to the high-flying stocks of recent years: Facebook, Amazon, Netflix, and Google.

27 Michael Lippert, as quoted in: Lewis Braham, "Growth vs. Value: More Divided Than Ever," *Barron's* (March 17, 2018), https:// www.barrons.com/articles/growth-vs-value-more-divided-than -ever-1521250404.

28 Bloomberg Finance LP, 2018, www.bloomberg.com.

29 The Bahnsen Group, www.thebahnsengroup.com.

30 If you noticed that these three components, the major embodiments of high inflation, are also the three most notorious recipients of government subsidy and intervention, you are astute.

31 Tim McMahon, "Gold and Inflation," InflationData.Com, April 25, 2018, https://inflationdata.com/Inflation/Inflation_Rate/Gold_ Inflation.asp.

32 "Even Modest Inflation Can Erode Purchasing Power," Pimco, https://www.pimco.com/en-us/resources/education/even-modest -inflation-can-erode-purchasing-power.

33 Annie Lowrey, "Are Stock Buybacks Starving the Economy?," *The Atlantic* (July 31, 2018).

34 Ibid.

35 This illustration makes no statement about the price performance of this dividend equity portfolio. It is only demonstrating the year-over-year growth of the actual dividend income.

36 "Income Yield on Original Investment Calculator," Miller/Howard Investments, https://tools.mhinvest.com/mhichart.

37 A reference to the top 10% and top 20% of yield level offered in the S&P 500. The caveat, of course, is that the yield is defined as *last dividend payment divided by current stock price.*

38 Howard Silverblatt, "2017 Year in Review," Standard & Poor's, August 2018.

39  Investment Strategy, Strategas Research, August 2017.

40  Ajay Kapur, Bank of America Merrill Lynch, Global Research Office, June 13, 2016.